reDefinition

Has the American Church correctly defined Christianity?

By
Matthew Clark

VIDE

Scripture quotations marked CSB have been taken from the Christian Standard Bible®, Copyright © 2017 by Holman Bible Publishers. Used by permission. Christian Standard Bible® and CSB® are federally registered trademarks of Holman Bible Publishers.

Vide Press
6200 Second Street
Washington D.C. 20011
www.VidePress.com

ISBN: 978-1-954618-18-3 (Print)
ISBN: 978-1-954618-19-0 (ebook)

Printed in the United States of America

Cover by Miblart.com

For my children. This is my letter to you.
The greatest thing I can do in my life is
to accurately show you who I live for.
I serve a Savior who loves me more
than I could ever imagine.

I desperately want you to know Him.

Table of Contents

Acknowledgments

The passion to write a book came later in my life. Having gone to school for music, I never imagined God would put me in this situation. As unqualified and underprepared as I felt when God laid this book concept on my heart, He surrounded me with the people who helped make it possible.

To my wife, Brittany. This would not have happened without your encouragement and support. God put you in my life to help me stay grounded and to keep my eyes on Him. Thank you for spending so many hours listening to me speak my thoughts. Thank you for holding down the house while I worked on this project at the library. Thank you for all the ideas you contributed to this book. I love you more than you will ever know.

Thank you to my in-laws, who allowed me to marry Brittany. I want to thank my parents who raised me in a godly home. Christ has been a central part of my life because my mom and dad showed He was real in theirs. Thank you, Dad, for showing me a great example of what a godly man looks like. Mom, I can't wait to see you again.

I would like to thank Cindy Graham and Rebecca Clark for making me sound a lot better than I really do. I appreciate the hours you put into this project. Thank you to Terri Foltz for giving me honest feedback on how to properly articulate my thoughts. Thank you to my friend, Kyubum Kim. This whole idea came about after a discussion we had at lunch. In all honesty, I probably owe you some royalties. I want to thank my close friends, Josh Velilla, Keith Beck, and Chris McLaughlin. We have had so many discussions about God and the world. Those discussions have had such a great impact on me. Thank you to Pastor Frank. I have loved every minute of working at the ministry that God has allowed you to lead. Thank you to Jeff Parker, from Vide Press, for taking my phone call, listening to my pitch, and deciding to work with me. And thank you to anyone that I did not mention. You have my permission to yell at me.

1:

We Have a Problem

"There is no use having a silent God. We would not know anything about Him."

Francis Schaeffer

The first step to finding a solution is to accurately define and diagnose the problem. You cannot get better if you do not acknowledge that you are sick. By any objective standard, one can see the United States of America is sick. Furthermore, you cannot get the correct answers if you are not asking the correct questions. The question is not "IS there a problem in the United States?" The question is "WHAT is the problem in the United States?"

I am troubled by what I see today. I look around and see the most prosperous nation in the history of the world falling apart. We are ripping at the seams, and the worst part is that this dilemma has not been brought about by some foreign power in the distance; it is happening from within. We have no one to blame but ourselves.

It brings a deep sense of grief when I see what we have become: so much hate, so little compassion. We have become a nation defined by division. Every issue, every single one, has become politicized.

As I write these words, our cities are burning from the riots brought on by the death of George Floyd. Our citizens have been forced into choosing a side: support the police or stand with the Black Lives Matter movement. This is a conversation that our country desperately needs to have, but instead, most have drawn a line in the sand and chosen a side. End of discussion. It is no longer about the exchange of ideas; it is about winning the argument.

Has this not become the case with most topics? Are you a Democrat or a Republican? A conservative or a liberal? Do you fight for the lives of unborn babies or a woman's right to choose? Are you for big government or small government? Do you kneel or stand for the National Anthem? While many of these arguments are not new, the amount of vitriol for the opposing side is. Unfortunately, I fear that the only time in our nation's history that mirrors what we see today is the Civil War.

Is this the problem we face in the United States? Disagreement? I believe it is beyond that. A differing opinion over a topic is not a terrible thing in itself. We can be united while having differing views. The problem does not lie in the abundance of division but rather in the absence of unity. There is a difference. I know two brothers who support opposing football teams which results in hostility during rivalry week. However, they are still united in the fact that they are family. Their bond as siblings is stronger than their disagreement. Do we forget that we are called the UNITED States? It used to be that simply being an American was what unified every citizen in this country. This is no longer the case. Sadly, our disagreements have come to define our relationships with others.

MISREPRESENTING CHRIST

What can bring unification and bridge this divide? Is it even possible for us to stop looking at the other side with disdain? Is there a way to love those whom we adamantly oppose? Christianity has the answer to this question: the most unifying aspect of every person alive is that we are made in the image of God. Even better is that a loving God died in our place for those who bear that image. That is what joins us together. That is what should unify us. Christians know this, but sadly, many believers keep it to themselves. They do not say a word.

In this desert we call life, the majority of people walk around trying to quench their thirst by clinging to the things of this world. They turn to the pursuit of fame, fortune, or relationships, unaware that these things will never fully satisfy. Christians, on the other hand, know the true source of life: Jesus is the living water that will sustain and the well that will never run dry. Why, then, do so many Christians hold this water in their hands and never share it with the thirsty? It is truly heartbreaking to realize that instead of showing non-believers the one thing that will save them, we keep it to ourselves as they die right in front of us of spiritual dehydration.

This is not the image of Christianity we see in the Bible. Suppressing the good news, or the Gospel, was not the lifestyle of the early Church. In the book of Acts, Luke details an unstoppable movement that happened solely because these Christians could not keep their mouths shut about what they knew. Their lifestyles matched the message they were sharing. In the United States, not only do many Christians abstain from proclaiming the truth of Christ, they live lifestyles that contradict the Gospel.

In 1 Peter 2:1, we are told that Christians are to *"rid yourselves of all malice, all deceit, hypocrisy, envy, and all slander."* Peter describes an image we are to strive for. In simple terms, those who love Christ should not portray these sinful attributes. It seems to me that many believers today have either not read this passage or simply ignored it.

I read the results of a survey once which left me discouraged. The question on the survey was, "What word would you use to describe Christians?" It would have been great to have seen loving, joyful, peaceful, and kind: all the fruits of the Spirit. Sadly, that did not happen. The top three words were hypocritical, judgmental, and homophobic.

Let me first say that the truth of the Gospel is offensive. Claiming that Jesus is the only way to heaven often offends people. There will be times when you share Jesus in the most loving and gentle way but will still be seen as hateful or judgmental. However, I do not think the results of that survey were based on interactions with loving and gentle Christians. Have you ever met a person who hates religion? Most times that hatred and disdain come from an experience they had with someone who claimed to love Jesus yet acted the way Peter instructed us not to. Should we expect the lost to turn to Christ when we misrepresent Him? It is as Gandhi once said, "I like your Christ, I do not like your Christians. Your Christians are so unlike your Christ."

Do you love people the way Jesus did?

Do you see sin the way Jesus did?

Is your primary motivation in life to act like Christ?

In his book *The Great Evangelical Recession*, John S. Dickerson predicts the future of the American Church based on the trends he sees today. This schism within the church is growing and will only get worse as the younger generation of believers buys into ideas that are not supported by Scripture.

> We may see postmodern subjectivity and pluralism blended more and more with evangelical theology, practice, and politics. This will be done more informally than formally. Old heresies will resurface as exciting new ideas. Inerrancy will be doubted and written off by some younger evangelicals who will mean well as they lead churches into that deadly error.[1]

---

1 Dickerson, John. *The Great Evangelical Recession*, p. 78.

D.A. Carson pointed out that "there are many people today who call themselves evangelical whom no person would call an evangelical 40 years ago." This is not to say that the sermons being preached forty years ago were perfect. What I am trying to communicate is that the American Church is preaching different messages: some biblical, some unbiblical. The place where unity should be most evident is within the body of Christ. Not only unity in fellowship with one another, but unity in message. Unity in proclaiming the truth.

I hate to say that the Christianity I see in our country today is very different from the Good News preached in other parts of the world. If you want proof of this, look to China and Iran: two of the most hostile places for believers. Yet, people are turning to Jesus at unbelievable rates. They are turning to Christ at the risk of losing everything; their families and often their lives.

Why is this not happening in the United States? The answer is simple: we are not showing them a Savior worth living or dying for.

In his book *Church of Cowards*, Matt Walsh begins by titling his first chapter, "Christians not worth killing." He tells a hypothetical story of a heathen horde that shows up to the shores of America intent on butchering some Christians for what they believe. Throughout the chapter, he describes what the American Church looks like today. How there is a consumeristic attitude of Americans while choosing a church to attend. How there are many "Christians" living hypocritical lifestyles every day of the week except Sundays.

After observing what Christianity has become, the heathen horde sailed away without killing a single person. Listen to the reason:

> Sorrowfully, gloomily, they walk back to their boats and sail away. They were not able to crush our Christian way of life—because we don't have a Christian way of life. They were not able to destroy the church because there wasn't much of a church left in America to destroy. They were not

able to behead the Christians because they couldn't find Christians to behead. They unsheathed their swords only to discover that what they came to kill was already dead. They had traveled all that way to persecute a corpse.[2]

Can we really blame unbelievers for how they view Christianity when they have not been given an accurate solution to their spiritual dilemma? We claim to follow Jesus, yet we commit some of the same sinful acts with no remorse. It is hard for me to have any ill will toward non-believers acting in sinful ways because this is how they act. We cannot hold people to godly standards if they do not know Christ. We should, however, hold each other accountable when we misrepresent Him.

WHO IS TO BLAME?

This is the difficult first question that we need to answer honestly. Are the preachers to blame or are the church members and congregations to blame? The answer is yes. Many pastors tell people what they want to hear instead of what they need to hear. Many churchgoers attend church simply for the "worship experience", having no real interest in living for Christ full-time. How many people attending church are unable to even share the Gospel, the foundation of our faith?

This is a failure that we all need to own. The first step of a recovering alcoholic is to admit they have a problem. This is difficult to do in the United States; We do not like to admit when we are wrong. We do not like to acknowledge failure. We do not like to ask for help. Many Christians are not interested in changing the way things have always been.

Is it possible that many Christians have been seeing Scripture as something it is not? Is the problem in what God says or what we

---

2   Walsh, Matt. *Church of Cowards*, p. 10.

have interpreted God to say? It is my opinion that so many American Christians do not see what Scripture really communicates leading to an inaccurate view of Jesus and Christianity.

DIFFERENT DEFINITIONS

It is not unusual for the meaning of a word to change over time. At some point in history, the word "nice" was not the compliment we know it as today. It used to mean "silly, foolish, or simple." The word "awful" was used to describe something as "worthy of praise." You were full of awe.

Words that have a change in meanings, such as these, do not typically cause any kind of stir or disagreement. However, there are cases of redefinition that divide. I recently read a news article about a college graduate from Missouri who penned a letter to the publisher of the Merriam-Webster dictionary. She felt that the dictionary needed an updated definition of the word "racism."

Merriam-Webster's definition of the word was, "A belief that race is the primary determinant of human traits and capacities and that racial differences produce an inherent superiority of a particular race." Seeing that the definition was lacking, the college student said, "Racism is not only prejudice against a certain race due to the color of a person's skin, as it states in your dictionary. It is both prejudice combined with social and institutional power. It is a system of advantage based on skin color."

Our country is currently in a heated debate over the topic of race, so one can see why this suggested redefinition would lead to arguments. This is even the case within the church. There is contention over which definition is accurate.

The chance of division goes up with the boldness of the claim. This happened in 1514 when Polish scientist, Nicolaus Copernicus, made the proposition that the Earth was not the center of the universe but that the planets revolved around the sun. This was obviously very contested as everyone defined the Earth as the central, most important thing in the universe. He was accused of heresy by the Catholic Church.

I have a friend who reminds me often that having clear definitions is important. Anytime we debate a subject, he says, "Define your terms." We cannot come to any kind of agreement or make any kind of progress if we do not agree on the meanings of words. How do you debate the topic of racism with someone when you have different opinions of what racism is? What happens when you see red and someone else sees green? Can two people agree on what is true if they define truth differently? That is where the problem lies. Regarding Scripture and what it teaches, I believe that many Christians have incorrectly defined the terms.

Seeing Scripture wrong means you see God and the world wrong. This has led to disastrous ideas within the Church. At one time in our country, the Bible was used to justify the ill-treatment of slaves. Other times, people use Scripture as a justification to point the finger at those living in sin. It is of the utmost importance that believers see what God is telling us through Scripture. We must stop misreading what He has said.

WHAT WOULD PAUL SAY?

I considered two titles as I began writing this book. The runner-up was "Americans: An Epistle to the church in America." All of Paul's epistles were written to different churches with instruction, encouragement, and correction. I often think about what Paul would say to the American Church today. I have a feeling his words would cut deep. I have a feeling we might not like what he would have to say.

How would Paul respond to how we treat unbelievers?

How would he respond to the tolerance of sin within our daily lives?

How would he respond to our lack of spiritual growth?

How would he respond to the priority placed on politics over faith?

You are probably familiar with the parable of the wise builder. Jesus tells the story in Matthew 7 about one man who built his house on the sand, while the other built his house on the rock.

> *Therefore, everyone who hears these words of mine and acts on them will be like a wise man who built his house on the rock. The rain fell, the rivers rose, and the winds blew and pounded the house. Yet it didn't collapse, because its foundation was on the rock. But everyone who hears these words of mine and doesn't act on them will be like a foolish man who built his house on the sand. The rain fell, the rivers rose, the winds blew and pounded that house, and it collapsed. It collapsed with a great crash.* (**Matthew 7:24–27**), **CSB.**

Is there a line in this parable that stands out to you? The verse that jumped off the page to me was, "*Everyone who hears these words of mine and does them will be like the wise man who built his house on the rock.*" Many so-called believers within the American Church simply do not do what our scriptures teach. It is hard to build a house if you do not read the blueprints.

I believe the problem lies within the first step: "*Everyone who hears these words of mine.*" One can only grow closer to God when hearing

His words. Do you accept what the Bible says, or are you putting meaning into the Scripture that is not there? When God says "stand," do you hear "sit"?

My wife once asked me to help my four-year-old clean the living room before dinner. He was still learning how to do chores and needed a little assistance. We knocked it out in five minutes, or so I thought. As we were about to sit down to eat, my wife looked at the living room and asked why we had not finished cleaning it. She began pointing out the different areas I missed. There were movies lying out on the TV stand. I did not vacuum. The shoes were not put away. Apparently, our definitions of the word "clean" were different.

Having been married to her for thirteen years, I should have known what she meant when she said "clean". Knowing my wife should have determined the meaning behind what she asked me to do. I am sure there are other wives who define "clean" differently, but that is not my business. I am only concerned with my wife's definition of the word.

Is the American Church more concerned with the way God defines things or our own definitions? Redefinition is a problem that the Church has created. It is a problem that the Church needs to fix. If Paul were to write an epistle today, I believe he would voice his disappointment in how we interpret what God has said in His Word. Francis Shaeffer points out that we only know God because He is not silent. He tells us who He is. It is up to us to see Him as He wants to be seen.

It is discouraging to see how Scripture passages can be heard or read incorrectly. It is like the old children's game of telephone. You sit in a circle and whisper the word to the person sitting next to you. Throughout the game, the original word gets mutilated and passed around so that when it gets to the last child, it is something completely different. It sounds nothing like what the first child said. Can you see this happening today?

In Luke 11:9, it says, "Ask and it will be given to you." The context of this passage tells us that when we ask for God to meet our needs in accordance with His will, then it will be given. How many things do we ask for out of selfish desire? People frequently hear this verse differently than it was intended. It has been passed around and mutilated leading people to think God will give them anything they ask for, as long as they do it in faith. As this passage is passed around within churches, being misheard and not fully explained, it is no wonder many Christians have an inaccurate understanding of Scripture.

Incorrectly reading the Bible leads to a false view of Jesus. So many of us look at the Bible through the lens of our culture and world today. This lens causes us to see God as something He is not, leading us to overlook what God is clearly telling us. If left unattended, these views can be disastrous for the upcoming generations.

When studying the Bible, authorial intent is of the utmost importance. Our opinions on the passage do not matter; it is what the author is telling us that matters. This is a practice called Exegesis. The opposite is called Eisegesis. This is when the reader places meaning into a text that the author did not intend.

Over time, I am convinced that we have given incorrect meanings to certain words and phrases in the Bible. The purpose of this book is to show the original definition of certain terms that have been redefined incorrectly. It is to promote the supremacy of Scripture. It is to push every reader to the realization that understanding the Bible correctly and implementing that truth is the most important aspect of our lives. God wants us to hear Him, but more importantly, He wants us to know Him.

There are seven terms from the Bible that I believe have been redefined and need to reclaim their original definition. My hope is that we can see what God originally intended these words to mean and that we can turn away from the incorrect meanings they have acquired. The seven terms are:

Truth (What is the standard by which you live your life?)

Belief (What truly leads to salvation?)

Sin (Does it matter if we offend God?)

Worship (Does your lifestyle show that God is worthy?)

Love (How are we to treat other believers?)

Evangelism (Does your faith exist outside the church walls?)

Abundant Life (What should one expect of the Christian life?)

BODY IMAGE

I want to be clear that I do not believe every Christian in the United States is guilty of redefining what the Bible says. I know many believers who faithfully live their lives by the Word of God. The problem I want to address lies within the diversity of the message coming from the body of Christ. There is an image being projected that I believe the early Church would reject. We have a "Church Body-Image" problem.

I once met a missionary who was visiting the United States. She came to our summer camp and spoke to the kids about some of the things she had seen on the mission field. We were all sitting around the campfire listening to every word about what God was doing in her life. She had witnessed things that could only be described as miraculous.

I was later able to have a one-on-one conversation with her. After hearing her talk, I could not help but wonder why these things were not happening here in America. When I asked what she thought, she responded by saying, "In my country, Jesus is not known yet. God has allowed these amazing things to happen to show who He is. It's no question that God has revealed Himself abundantly in America. It seems to me that most people just aren't listening." I will never forget what she said next: "I think our countries see Jesus differently.

In fact, I think the churches within the United States see Jesus differently from one another."

There is a lot of truth in what she said. We have elevated our minor differences making our major agreements secondary. Did you know that there are both Christian Republicans and Democrats? Are you aware that Christians can disagree over the age of the Earth without being heretical or anti-scientific? I am not saying that we should not discuss and debate these issues within the Church family. Defending your position makes you stronger in your faith. But whether we know it or not, our division within the Church has now defined us to those looking in from the outside. These in-house issues and fights have hindered the spread of the Gospel. The image we are putting out is a house divided.

Focusing on our differences internally has kept our vision inward instead of focusing outward to those who desperately need to hear the message of salvation. This is the question that needs answering: What are the primary things in Christianity that we should all believe? These are the things we should be projecting to non-believers. We need to start answering the questions that matter. We need to start focusing on the issues that affect salvation. I find it sad that so many people within the church are more evangelical about their politics than their faith.

We serve one God who has given us one Word. He is not different based on the country you live in. The Church in America needs to unify over the truth of the Bible. God desires that we see the world through the lens of Scripture. C.S. Lewis put it perfectly: "I believe in Christianity as I believe that the sun has risen. Not only because I see it, but because by it I see everything else." Let us see God, His Word, and life the way He intended us to.

TAKE ACTION

Find another Christian that disagrees with you and take them to lunch. The disagreement can be over politics, theological matters, social issues, etc. Allow the conversation to happen without getting angry. Try and find areas of agreement. The entire point of the conversation is to find unity amid disagreement.

IN REVIEW

1. The problem does not lie in the abundance of division but rather in the absence of unity.

2. The most unifying aspect of every person alive is that they are made in the image of God.

3. Instead of showing non-believers the one thing that will save them, we keep it to ourselves as they die, right in front of us, of spiritual dehydration.

4. We cannot come to any kind of agreement or make any kind of progress if we do not agree on the meanings of words.

5. If Paul were to write an epistle today, I believe he would voice disappointment in how we interpret what God has said in His Word.

6. Incorrectly reading the Bible leads to a false view of Jesus.

7. We have a "Church Body-Image" problem.

8. We have elevated our minor differences making our major agreements secondary.

9. We need to start answering the questions that matter.

10. God desires that we see the world through the lens of Scripture.

Nothing but the Truth So Help Me God

reDefined: Truth

*"The truth is still the truth even if no one believes it.
A lie is still a lie, even if everyone believes it."*

Unknown

---

*Do not be conformed to this age, but be transformed by the
renewing of your mind, so that you may discern what is the
good, pleasing, and perfect will of God.* (**Romans 12:2**)**, CSB.**

WHAT I FEAR MOST

Everyone is scared of something. Some polls show the top three fears
to be heights, spiders/snakes, and public speaking. I realized what
I am most scared of a couple of years ago when I was sitting in my
living room watching *The Empire Strikes Back*. As I was enjoying my
favorite scene (when Darth Vader tells Luke that he is his father),
I noticed a small black circle fall from the curtain and begin flying

laps around my living room. It was a bat. I broke into a cold sweat, dropped to the floor, and crawled to my wife who was in the kitchen.

It was the first time I realized how much bats terrify me. At that moment, there was nothing I was scared of more. However, I can now admit that, in the grand scheme of things, bats are really not that bad. There are scarier things to be afraid of. What is your worst fear?

Thankfully, the year 2020 has come and gone. I once heard someone refer to it as "the year of fear." This is an appropriate title as many people's fears came to fruition. In years prior, scientists were concerned that a global pandemic could happen. That fear became reality. Imagine what a parent would have said if you told them that they would be locked up with their children for six months? That scenario would terrify any parent. Covid-19 made that happen.

There is something, though, that I see happening which terrifies me more than anything. I fear that our country is losing its grasp on truth. Look around and see if you agree. Which news station is reporting the facts? Is your college professor teaching truth or giving a biased opinion? We are living in a time now where we trust or distrust a politician based on their party affiliation. Truth has become subjective. It changes based upon who you talk to.

I am reminded of the passage in Scripture where Jesus was brought before Pilate.

> *Then Pilate went back into the headquarters, summoned Jesus, and said to him, "Are you the king of the Jews?" Jesus answered, "Are you asking this on your own, or have others told you about me?" "I'm not a Jew, am I?" Pilate replied. "Your own nation and the chief priests handed you over to me. What have you done?" "My kingdom is not of this world," said Jesus. "If my kingdom were of this world, my servants would fight, so that I wouldn't be handed over to the Jews. But as it is, my kingdom*

is not from here." "You are a king then?" Pilate asked. "You say that I'm a king," Jesus replied. "I was born for this, and I have come into the world for this: to testify to the truth. Everyone who is of the truth listens to my voice." "What is truth?" said Pilate. (John 18:33–38), CSB.

As Jesus was telling Pilate the purpose of His life, Pilate responded with ignorance: "What is truth?" Can you blame him though? He had lived his entire life believing in what some call the imperial cult (emperors of Rome and members of their families were seen as gods). Jesus was telling Pilate of a truth he had never heard before.

This passage is extremely relevant for what we face today. The reality of our current society is that there is competition as to which "truth" is real. Our culture tells us that there are many truths a person can choose from. What happens if one "truth" contradicts another? There are worldviews people subscribe to that are in complete opposition to each other. Who is right? What is true?

WHAT IS TRUTH?

How can we know what is true? The scientific method and advances in technology have allowed us to grow in our knowledge. As time goes on, we will find that we were wrong about certain things and have to adjust how we think. Humanity has made marvelous strides in scientific discovery. Does this mean that truth has changed over time or that we are simply growing closer to what truth really is?

Before we go any further, I first want to define what I mean when I speak of truth. If we are not careful, we can fall into the trap of believing that truth is still being discovered. This is why it is important to distinguish between truth and knowledge. Christians should have no problem when the scientific method reveals something we did not know. Truth must be something more. It is a step beyond knowledge.

The truth an individual believes is the lens by which he/she sees the world. Every decision and every action is rooted in that truth.

The lens by which the believer sees the world is Scripture. Truth is taken from the Word of God. Everything that happens should be filtered through what the Bible says. If you do not know what to think about something, look to Scripture. If you struggle with a certain moral dilemma, turn to the Bible. If you do not know which politician to vote for, compare their policies to what God says. In her book *Total Truth*, Nancy Pearcey says that seeing things through a Christian lens "means understanding that Christianity gives the truth about the whole of reality, a perspective for interpreting every subject matter."[3]

The Word of God is an unchanging truth that never wavers. I wonder if many of us in the Church are turning to the "truths" of our time and forgetting that our standard is the Word of God. Have we allowed the truth to be redefined?

One of the most destructive statements of our time is, "Live your truth." The idea is that an individual should only pursue the things that make them happy, even at the expense of others. Earthly happiness has taken the place of God's Word and caused people to turn to worldly things for a sense of fulfillment. I read a story recently of a mother who left her family and pursued a homosexual lifestyle. She claimed that she got married too early in life and missed out on the opportunity of sexual exploration. Living "her truth" meant the abandonment of her family.

Do not think this happens only outside the Church. Many believers do not live by the truth of Scripture. Christianity has become a very convenient religion as many Christians are living out half a faith. Jesus is not their foundation anymore. If you allow things like tradition and preference to take the place of Christ, you are living out "your truth" and not the truth the Bible speaks of.

---

3 Pearcey, Nancy. *Total Truth*, p. 34.

Can these kinds of "truths" really be called good? This kind of thinking is utterly subjective, defining truth as something that is constantly changing and determined by feelings. This destructive mindset leads to an inevitable contradiction. What if your earthly happiness conflicts with someone else's? Who is right? Who is wrong?

It used to be that a person could say "1+1=2" and there would be no discussion about it. Our culture now tells us that if someone disagrees with that answer and says "1+1=4", we are to accept what they are saying because it is true to them. We do not have to agree, but we are supposed to keep that disagreement to ourselves. It is actually worse, in that the same person can come up to you the very next day and say they now believe "1+1=5," completely changing their answer because they want it to be different.

It is puzzling that two different pregnant women can have opposing views as to what is inside their wombs. One mother can say it is a baby that she will one day give birth to and love with all her heart. The other can say that the fetus is merely a sack of cells that she can discard; It is a part of her body and she can do as she wants.

How can we look at these two ladies and accept both answers as truth? If a mother is on her way to an abortion clinic and gets stabbed, killing the baby, is it homicide? We cannot let feelings be the basis for what is true.

The danger of determining truth by feelings is that truth has now become extremely selfish. A person is told that truth can be anything they want it to be. Sometimes the best thing is for a person to hear the hard truth making them feel bad or uncomfortable. Have you ever looked in the mirror and realized it is time to go on a diet?

WHAT DO YOU LIVE FOR?

The easiest way to determine what you consider to be truth is to recognize what you live for. If everyone was to examine themselves, they would see that there is something that motivates them. There is something they consider to be worth fighting for. The United States has no shortage of charitable organizations. Some feed the hungry. Some give clothes to the homeless. Some people, like Dr. Martin Luther King Jr., dedicated their lives to civil rights.

These are all good and noble acts. However, the reason for doing them is what makes the difference. Dr. Martin Luther King Jr. fought for the rights of minorities not simply because he wanted equality. He fought for these rights because the Bible was his standard of truth and the Bible states that we are to love one another, no matter the color of our skin.

For the believer, the Word of God is what determines our purpose. It is what dictates our actions and motivations in life. The Scripture is not merely a book that contains stories and moral advice. The Bible is literally the Words of God. Augustine once said that "when the Bible speaks, God speaks." There is one truth, and it comes from God. We cannot let culture determine what truth is.

I believe this to be the root of the spiritual decline we are seeing in the United States. I am not surprised to see the culture turning away from God. I am surprised, however, at the number of Christians who proclaim Christ but do not live for Him. I am also surprised at the number of Christians who have silenced the voice of God in their lives by keeping their Bibles closed. If what Augustine said is true, many Christians are daily choosing to never hear from God. It is no wonder that our culture wants nothing to do with God because so many Christians have the same mentality.

To live out the truth, we first have to know the truth. The Devil is doing everything in his power to stop believers from living on mission for Christ. Unfortunately, he has been successful in deceiving Christians that the Bible does not hold the importance it should, causing us to ignore God's Word. This is nothing new. The Devil has been deceiving since the beginning of time in the Garden of Eden. For this reason, we need to always be on guard and in the Word.

Imagine you are walking down the street and some guy wants to sell you a painting. He tells you it is the Mona Lisa. Not a replica, but the original, authentic Mona Lisa. You have heard that this painting is famous, and you could use some artwork on your bare apartment walls. The man makes you a great offer and you cannot believe your luck.

When you get home, you put it up on your wall and invite your artsy friends over to marvel at your new purchase. One of your friends, let us call him Steve, pulls you away from the group. Steve reveals to you that the painting hanging on your wall is not the original Mona Lisa. Not wanting to believe him, you ask Steve how he knows. He tells you that he had to do a project on the Mona Lisa and studied it. He knows exactly how it is supposed to look. Steve then walks over to the painting on your wall and points to the bottom corner. He points out that the coloring is wrong. The real Mona Lisa is colored differently. You see, Steve only knows that the picture is fake because he knows what the original looks like.

Paths are only crooked when you know how straight paths are supposed to look. Make no mistake, the Devil is trying to deceive us every chance he gets. He is a master at taking something true and altering it ever so slightly, thus making it a deception. We have to be on guard. For us to know when we are being deceived by the devil, we need to know what the truth looks like first. This will only happen if we are hearing the truth regularly from God's Word.

DO NOT WAVER

Think about everything Jesus went through. Those who opposed Him had Him killed. His closest friends abandoned Him in His greatest time of need. People questioned and doubted Him. All of these things are enough for a person to throw in the towel, but Jesus was different. Standing before the courts, being accused of blasphemy, He could have spoken up and avoided the physical punishment He eventually endured. But He did not. Was it because He could not stop it? Jesus answers this question with another question in Matthew 26:53. *"Do you think that I cannot call on my Father, and He will provide me here and now with more than twelve legions of angels?"* Clearly, Jesus could have prevented all the hardships He experienced, but He allowed them to happen anyway. Why?

As far as I can see, there were three reasons: (1) **Jesus had a mission that He came to fulfill, and He would let nothing stand in His way**. He would not and did not waver. Have you ever met a person who was so focused and passionate about something they set their mind to? Jesus knew His purpose for walking the earth.

(2) **He trusted the Father**. His faith in God's plan was unbreakable because He knew God was in control. I remember a time when I was a teenager helping out in the children's ministry of my church. My friend and I put together a short play that was *Star Wars* themed. We wrote the script and even choreographed the scenes using lightsabers we made. During one of our rehearsals, we were going over a scene that involved me dropping to the ground as my friend swung his lightsaber. As I began to drop, he started swinging too soon, hitting me in the back of the head. Getting hit in the head with a wooden lightsaber is extremely painful. He apologized and we tried again. Unfortunately, the result was the same.

At this point, I thought it would be a good idea to rewrite the scene so I could avoid getting hit for a third time, but my friend insisted we get it right. He assured me that it would not happen again; however,

I had no faith in my friend. I had no reason to trust him because he gave me no reason to trust him.

Jesus was in a different situation. He showed that we can have faith and trust in the Father because He never lets us down. The Bible is full of promises that God fulfills in our lives over and over again. We have every reason to trust God because He has not given us a reason to doubt Him.

(3) **Jesus had a fixed point of reference**. In Matthew 4, Jesus is tempted in the wilderness by the Devil. He is literally promised everything one could ever desire; yet He overcame everything the Devil threw at Him. In fact, Jesus responded to the lies the Devil used with the truth of Scripture. It makes sense, doesn't it? The Devil lies but the Word of God is truth. Jesus was able to withstand the temptations because He stood firm in the truth of God.

Frank Peretti, a Christian fiction author, spoke at a church once about the importance of having a fixed point of reference regarding the truth. Whatever it is that you follow, whatever you consider to be truth, should be something that remains steady. It should not change. Peretti illustrated this point with a chair. When you are about to sit down, you want the chair to stay in a fixed position. Have you ever seen a person fall over when the chair was pulled out from underneath them?

We should want that same consistency from the truth we follow. As I write this chapter, I am sitting in a chair in my dining room. When I sat down, I was confident that my chair would be in the exact spot and not move. I have that same confidence in the Word of God. Why? Because God is the same yesterday, today, and tomorrow (Hebrews 13:8). He does not change. When Scripture says something about God, we can trust that truth to remain firm.

This is not the case with other "truths" of our time. Like I discussed earlier, truth has become subjective; it changes based on feelings.

A person following a subjective truth is not following a point of reference that is fixed; it is variable. Believe me when I say that this is an awful way to live. Imagine having no confidence as you are about to sit down on a chair because there is a chance it might move on you. You cannot be sure it is going to be in the same spot. People who follow variable truths will eventually find themselves lying flat on their backs because their "truth" has left them behind.

Finding a fixed point of reference, however, is only half of it. We should not simply be looking for a truth that does not waver; we need to avoid wavering ourselves. The Devil is very aware of the fact that, while God cannot be moved, it is often very easy to move us. It is as if you are about to sit down on the unwavering chair that never moves, and as you are doing so, another chair catches your eye off to the side. Yes, you love the chair that you normally rest on, but that other chair looks really nice. It looks like it might be more comfortable. Before you know it, you have left your old chair behind.

This is the temptation of every Christian. We so easily forget that God's Word is the only truth we can rely on. "Truths," such as lust and wealth, lure us away with the assurance that they can support us. It is a lie and it always has been. I have been heartbroken over the number of Christian leaders that have recently had to step down over sinful decisions they have made. These are people I respected. They fell victim to the idea that there were other chairs worth sitting on. They wavered.

Oftentimes, Christians will turn to other "truths" with the mindset that they can better support them in their times of need. They believe that these "truths" will hold them up in their weariness. Fight this way of thinking. Do so by remembering all the saints that have come before us.

How many times in the Bible have we read about someone putting their trust in God against all logic? How about the time when God told Abram to leave his home without knowing where he was going

(Genesis 12:1)? The time when God limited Gideon's army to just 300 men (Judges 7)? The Apostle Paul's entire ministry?

We have so many examples of people placing their trust in God no matter what stood before them. They survived those hardships by relying on the strength of God, not their own. God can endure any weight that comes His way. He can endure yours. There is nothing you are going through that is too heavy for God. While other chairs may entice us away, know that the chair representing the truth of God, has not and will never break under the weight that rests on it.

MOVED BY SCIENCE

Before I move on, I want to address the chair that I believe has moved many people away from the Word of God: the reverence for science. I am amazed at the amount of religious attention science receives today. It has become a god to so many. It has caused people to walk away from the real God, becoming a barrier that stands in the way of salvation.

How a person defines science says a lot about how they view the world. I love the definition that Johannes Kepler gives: "Science is the process of thinking God's thoughts after him." When science is viewed this way, it is put in its proper place, as observation. Science is observing what God has done and making note of those observations. This is not the mantle on which science currently sits. It has become far more than observation. Our society has given science divinity.

This lie fits the mindset that our world has come to embrace: naturalism. Naturalism is defined as "the view of the world that takes account only of natural elements and forces, excluding the supernatural or spiritual."[4] If something cannot be explained scientifically, it is not seen as truth. This is the difference between

---

4 Dictionary.com

the natural and the supernatural. Supernatural events cannot be explained because they break the rules of nature.

As the definition above states, supernatural or spiritual explanations are excluded or discounted. This explains why so many scientists struggle with religion. If a process cannot be broken down to naturalistic observation, they simply say that we have not found the answer yet. They will not credit God because He cannot be proven naturalistically.

C.S. Lewis addresses this topic in his book *Mere Christianity*. He calls this view the Materialist view defining it as "those who think that matter and space just happen to exist, and always have existed, nobody knows why; and that the matter, behaving in certain fixed ways, has just happened, by a sort of fluke, to produce creatures like ourselves who are able to think."[5]

This way of thinking only tells us the "how" of the universe. It does not explain the "why." Science can tell us how a seed comes to be a flower, but it cannot tell us why stealing from someone is bad. Natural observation of the world, or science, does not tell us anything about morality. It cannot tell us what is right or wrong. No amount of science labs can determine whether or not the Cambodian genocide by the Khmer Rouge was evil. That is a moral discussion.

Lewis makes the argument that our morality has to be based on something outside of nature: "If there was a controlling power outside the universe, it could not show itself to us as one of the facts inside the universe—no more than the architect of a house could actually be a wall or staircase or fireplace in that house."[6]

Do you see the point he is making? The naturalist has no ground to stand on when speaking of right or wrong. The house does not determine morality, the builder does. The next time you are having

---

5   Lewis, C.S. *Mere Christianity*, p. 28.
6   Lewis, C.S. *Mere Christianity*, p. 30.

a discussion with a non-believer about morality, ask them the basis by which they believe. Without God, there is no answer. Do society and culture determine what is morally true? The answer is obviously no because different cultures see morality differently. Which ones are right and which ones are wrong?

I believe this explains the dire situation America is in today. Our country has fully embraced the idea that science can account for everything. Is it any wonder that America is falling apart morally? We have bought into the morally absent religion of science.

DOES SCIENCE CONTRADICT GOD?

A friend of mine was asked if he thought science contradicted God while preaching a sermon on Jonah. Jonah was the prophet that disobeyed God by avoiding His call. As a response, God allowed Jonah to be swallowed by a giant fish and taken to Nineveh, the place he was told to go (Jonah 1:17). For the naturalistic mind, this story is nonsensical. How does a man survive inside the stomach of a fish for three days?

This question was asked by a young man who sat through my friend's sermon. He struggled with this Bible passage because it seemingly contradicted science. There were several reasons why this man could not have realistically lived three days inside a fish. As he began to list them, my friend interrupted him:

> You know what, you're right. I can't explain scientifically how Jonah lived inside the fish. It was a supernatural event. However, what I can tell you is that I believe God created the universe simply by speaking it into existence. For me, believing a man lived inside a fish for three days isn't a stretch of the imagination. In comparison, it's actually pretty easy.

We should not shudder when we see parts of the Bible contradicting science. It simply means that God is beyond the laws of nature. He is not bound by these laws, because He created them. This is how He can speak things into existence. This is how Moses was able to part the Red Sea. This is how Jesus was able to walk on water and later be raised from the dead. None of these things can be explained scientifically.

Think about it. Even if my friend was able to present scientific data to support how Jonah could have survived, would it have changed anything? Would this knowledge alone have saved this young man? Christians fall into the trap of needing to explain everything scientifically, and in doing so, forget what really saves a person. This is not to say that Christians should abstain from scientific discussions. On the contrary, I believe our country needs more Christian scientists.

God has set natural laws into place and there is great benefit from learning as much as we can about how God chose to assemble the world. The point is that we should not be more eager to win an argument over teaching the Gospel. What Jesus did on the cross should be the thesis of every discussion with non-believers. How Jesus freed us from sin should saturate every aspect of our lives.

BE OFFENSIVE...

I was once having a discussion with one of my friends about politics. He brought up certain politicians that he neither liked nor respected. When I asked him why he felt this way, he told me that "he does not like politicians who are divisive."

I was confused by his statement. I can understand wanting more civility in government, but I made the point that being divisive is not necessarily a bad thing. For many people, this word has taken on a negative meaning, and I am not sure why. By simply speaking the truth, you run the risk of being divisive or offensive. It is not always malicious or mean.

For example, I remember a time when I was walking down the hallway of my church and crossed paths with my senior Pastor. I had not seen him in a couple of weeks, and he looked a little different. I could not put my finger on it. I said to him, "You look different. Have you gotten a tan?" He replied, "A tan? I'm not sure. I hadn't really noticed." "Well," I said, "either you got a tan, or your hair has gotten whiter."

I thought it was funny, but my pastor did not feel the same way. He is in his sixties and any references made to his age tend to get me in trouble. The reality of getting older was not a truth my pastor was interested in hearing.

We are living in a time where respecting feelings has taken over how we communicate with one another. Offending someone has become the unforgivable sin. The reality is that there are times people need to hear something offensive and difficult to hear. You should not be angry at the doctor giving a cancer diagnosis. He is merely informing you about something deadly.

I am amazed at how often we Christians keep our mouths shut when someone needs to hear the truth. When you have a person's well-being at heart, offensive statements can be the most loving things you say. The man hooked on drugs needs to hear that he is ruining his life. The father who never spends time with his children needs someone to tell him to step up. The young lady who gives herself sexually over and over again needs someone to tell her the truth about respecting herself.

These are not easy conversations to have. When people are captive to sin, they often justify their actions, and speaking the truth can be met with resistance. Therein lies the problem. Many Christians do not share the truth for fear of being offensive. We care more about people's feelings than we do about their souls. This has to change.

Did Jesus care about offending people? The Gospels show that Jesus did not seem to mind when people got upset hearing the truth.

He rebuked the Pharisees for being hypocrites (Matthew 23). He often talked about the seriousness of sin and how it leads to eternal punishment (Matthew 5:30). We have to remember that Jesus did not come to earth to make everyone feel good about themselves; He came to tell people what they needed to hear. He was not concerned in the slightest about being divisive or offensive. We see this in Matthew 10:34, *"Don't assume that I came to bring peace on the earth. I did not come to bring peace, but a sword."*

It was the passion of Jesus that drove Him. He cared so much about people that their feelings were secondary. Have you ever been passionate about something? Fans of a football team do not care who hears them cheer. Parents make statements like: "I have the cutest child in the world." They do not mind that other parents might disagree because they feel they have the cutest child in the world. Passion can lead us to overlook things that can be considered divisive.

BE OFFENSIVE ... IN LOVE

How you share the truth makes all the difference. Jesus had such a strong passion for people, and it showed in His words and His actions. We are called to live out the truth, not simply say it. People will only believe what we say if we live it out also. A lack of doing so is hypocrisy.

Unfortunately, hypocrisy has become attached to the perception of Christianity, and for good reason. Our actions always speak louder than our words. Have you ever met a person who left the church? A large percentage of them leave because of how they were treated by Christians. We are undermining our mission when our actions do not line up with our message.

We must share the truth the way Jesus did. Sadly, and I am guilty of this myself, speaking the truth often becomes more about winning the argument than the soul. It becomes about being right. I have had discussions with non-believing students in youth groups where we ended up arguing about spiritual issues. I specifically remember leaving one night, having "won" the argument but feeling terrible afterward. I had said all the right things, but I said them in a way that came across as over-confident. If I am being honest, my goal was to humiliate the student. It was to prove that her ideas were ignorant. She was getting angry with me, making me want to win the argument that much more.

Greg Koukl has a general rule when talking to someone about Jesus: "If anyone in the discussion gets angry, you lose."[7] If what he says is true, then I lost. I may not have lost the debate, but I lost the chance to show Jesus accurately. My words were offensive, but they were not offensive in love. We must remember that those who are blind to the truth are being deceived. This should cause us to alter our strategy in proclaiming the truth. Souls are literally on the line.

The most ironic thing about Pilot asking the question "What is truth?" is that he was literally looking truth in the eyes and did not even realize it. Jesus was standing before him and he missed it. I actually feel pity for Pilot, not anger.

We need to stop being mad at those who are being deceived by the Devil. They are lost and need the truth, not a lecture. We need to direct our anger to the deceiver and grieve the deceived. Think of the impact we could have on our country if we were to have compassion for those who do not know the truth.

TAKE ACTION

Make a list of the important truths of Christianity. After writing them down, practice saying them in a non-confrontational way as if you were having a conversation with a non-believer. Remember, the

---

7 Koukl, Greg. *Tactics*, p. 30.

very nature of the Gospel can be offensive to someone who does not know Christ. What is important is how you deliver the message. Is your proclamation Christ-like?

IN REVIEW

1. The reality of our current society is that there is a competition as to which "truth" is real.

2. The truth an individual believes is the lens by which he/she sees the world.

3. Earthly happiness has taken the place of God's Word and caused people to turn to worldly things for a sense of fulfillment.

4. The danger of determining truth by feelings is that truth has now become extremely selfish.

5. To live out the truth, we first have to know the truth.

6. We have every reason to trust God because He has not given us a reason to doubt Him.

7. The Devil is very aware of the fact that, while God cannot be moved, it is often very easy to move us.

8. Many Christians have bought into the morally absent religion of science.

9. Many Christians do not share the truth for fear of being offensive.

10. We need to direct our anger to the deceiver and grieve the deceived.

Identity Theft

reDefined: Belief

The first step in forming a Christian worldview is to overcome this sharp divide between "heart" and "brain."

Nancy Pearcey

If you confess with your mouth, "Jesus is Lord," and believe in your heart that God raised Him from the dead, you will be saved. (**Romans 10:9**), **CSB**.

HOW DO YOU BELIEVE?

Notice the question is not "Do you believe?". The emphasis is on the word "How." John 3:16 says, *"For God so loved the world, that he gave His only Son, that whoever believes in Him should not perish but have eternal life."* This is arguably the most famous scripture passage in the entire Bible. We are taught to memorize it in Sunday school, and even many non-Christians know this verse.

This passage shows us the heart of God. It shows us how far He was willing to go out of love for His people. What if I told you, though, that I believe John 3:16 has been heard incorrectly causing many to have an invalid faith? It is a bold claim.

Think for a moment, if you were in the Devil's shoes. How could you use this Scripture to steer people away from the Lord? It is a strange question since this passage preaches the gospel that leads to Salvation. If you believe in Jesus Christ, you will be saved. So how could this verse possibly be used to point people away from God? Unfortunately, the Devil has figured this out with a very high success rate. This deception hinges on the word "believe." How a person defines this word is the difference between being saved or not.

I was watching a debate once between a Christian and an atheist. As the debate was coming to an end, the moderator allowed the Christian one more opportunity to ask the atheist a question. He asked, "What would it take for you to believe in God? Is there anything that can happen, any evidence, that would lead you to Christ?" The atheist did not miss a beat. He leaned forward and spoke into the microphone: "If I was walking outside one day and looked up at the sky and saw a giant hand spell out in the clouds 'I am God and I am real', then maybe I would believe in God."

What the atheist said tells us exactly how the Devil has redefined the word "believe." He has convinced so many that it merely means "knowledge." If you believe with your mind that Jesus died for your sins, then you will go to heaven. This deception makes sense when you consider how our world has come to view science and evidence. If we believe the story of Jesus to be factual and sufficient, we label ourselves Christians.

In reality, it is not enough to believe the event of Jesus' death happened. Scholars have been debating for years whether Jesus Christ actually lived, died, and was resurrected. At this point, the consensus among both believers and non-believers is that He walked the earth and died on a cross. There is even solid evidence that many people witnessed Jesus after His death. Does believing any of those statements do anything for your soul?

The atheist from the debate was under the assumption that salvation hinges on knowledge. Even if the atheist stood face to face with God, would the mere comprehension of His existence be enough? The sad truth is that this deception is believed by so many churchgoers who think they are saved simply because they believe with their minds that God exists. Many people who claim to follow Christ have fallen victim to this redefinition.

BATMAN AND KIM JONG UN

A couple of years ago, I was given the opportunity to go on a mission trip to Cambodia. This is a country that, while beautiful, has been ravished by war and poverty. Having never been on a mission trip before, I jumped at the opportunity. The friend who invited me was part of an organization that founded Christian homes for orphaned children.

The welcome we received when we arrived was unlike anything I had ever experienced. As we pulled into the compound, the children were running alongside the van waving at us. When we stepped out of the vehicle, the children swarmed us with hugs and smiles. I had never felt more welcome in my life.

We spent the entire day getting to know the children. There were so many amazing stories of how God had saved these kids. As the day went on, a kid named Timothy approached me and began to ask me several questions about my family and where I was from. Our conversation went a different direction when he noticed the Batman logo that was on my shirt. Timothy had no idea who this superhero was, so I found it my duty to educate him on the greatest crime-fighter known to man.

I told him that the Dark Knight fights for justice and defends the innocent. He is the master detective who always has a plan. Batman is a good guy. However, I am not sure he fully understood what I was saying based on his next question: "Have you ever eaten dog?"

I had never experienced a transition like this before. To be honest, it took me off guard. I told him that in America we do not do that. We play with dogs, not eat them. This was not the case in Cambodia. For a lot of people, dog was the only meat they could eat because they could not afford anything else.

I told Timothy that he sounded a lot like Kim Jong Un (the only person I could think of at the moment who approved of eating dogs). In hindsight, this was a claim I wish I could have taken back. For those who are not familiar with Kim Jong Un, he is the dictator of North Korea and is no friend of the United States. In fact, he is not even a friend to his own people. He treats them horribly and starves them. Instead of feeding his people, he has convinced them that dog meat is a "super meat" and that everyone should eat it.

Timothy apparently had no idea who the dictator was because he looked at me with a thumbs up and asked, "Kim Jong Un is a good guy?" I quickly responded with a thumbs down saying, "No. Thumbs down. Kim Jong Un is not a good guy. He is a bad man. A really bad man." A smile then formed on Timothy's face. "Kim Jong Un is … Batman?" Realizing he misheard my comment, I went into panic mode. "No. Not Batman. A bad man. Bad man." Timothy kept his thumb up, "Kim Jong Un is Batman, a superhero."

I stood there in disbelief. What had I done? I walked over to the two friends I came with and said, "Gentlemen, I may have just inadvertently convinced a child that the dictator of North Korea is a superhero. I think it's time to go."

This story is obviously a funny example of what can go wrong when a language barrier is present. I had accidentally made a dictator appear to be something that he was not. Kim Jong Un is not a superhero. He does not fight for justice. However, while I did this on accident, dictators do this on purpose.

You can look throughout history and see many examples of this deception. They actively try to convince their people that they want what is best even though their actions contradict that claim. This is a form of identity theft: claiming to be something and then living a lifestyle that shows the opposite.

Identity theft, however, is not exclusively reserved for dictators. Many Christians are guilty of this same crime. They claim to be a believer yet live a life that contradicts that claim. In fact, there are several "Christians" (notice the quotation marks) who are committing identity theft and do not even realize it. They genuinely believe they are living godly lives but instead, do not even have a relationship with the Lord. This is one of the greatest tricks of the Devil: convincing people to subscribe to a counterfeit salvation. Convincing people that knowledge of God is the only requirement to be saved.

THE GREAT DECEPTION

The great deception is that there are Christians who do not even know they are committing identity theft. These are the ones who only have knowledge of God with no personal relationship. They have been tricked into believing that the knowledge of what Christ did on the cross is enough to save their soul. Say what you will about the Devil, you cannot deny how strategic this deception is. People have been tricked into believing they are spiritually secure. They have been tricked into thinking they have a relationship with Christ.

In his book *The Story of Reality*, Greg Koukl says:

The sad fact is, every Sunday, churches are filled with "believers" who are not Christians. There is nothing defective about their doctrine, yet they are still completely disconnected from God. They know about Jesus, they assent to Jesus, but they have never trusted in Jesus, and this is evident from the way they live their lives.[8]

A person has a chance of beating cancer when they know they have it. They are able to start treatment with the hope of healing. A person cannot be healed from cancer when they are not even aware it is spreading throughout their body.

ARE YOU INVOLVED OR COMMITTED?

Tim Elmore tells a great story of a Kamikaze pilot that shows what it means to be fully invested.

> I love this story of a kamikaze pilot who flew in World War II for the Japanese Air Force. He was interviewed by a newspaper reporter after returning from his fiftieth mission. The reporter asked the pilot if he wasn't a contradiction in terms. How can someone be a kamikaze pilot—whose mission is to fly into military bases and give up their life in the process—and still be alive after fifty missions? "Well, it's like this," the pilot responded. "I was very involved. Not very committed, but very involved."[9]

Committed Kamikaze's go on ONE mission. The pilot was not able to fully complete his task because he was not sold out to the cause. Churches are full of these kinds of people. Involvement is the main symptom of the "Christian" who is committing identity

---

8 Koukl, Greg. *The Story of Reality*, p. 135.
9 Elmore, Tim. *Habitudes*, p. 79.

theft. These are the ones who look at Christianity as a checklist of actions that need to be completed. Did I go to church this Sunday? Check. Did I raise my hands during worship? Check. Did I give my tithe? Check. Simply going through the motions is not evidence of commitment. It only shows involvement. Here are a couple of ways to assess yourself to see if you are merely involved.

Your faith is only seen on Sundays. Nowhere in Scripture are we told to live out our faith in particular time blocks. In 1 Corinthians 11:1, Paul tells us to *"be imitators of Christ."* This command is not given to only be completed on certain days. We are to imitate Jesus in every aspect of our lives with every breath and every thought. Imagine if a spouse only showed love and affection one day a week. Imagine they only showed their love on Valentine's Day. Does that marriage sound like it is going to last?

There is also a selfish aspect to this point. Involved Christians need to be seen. They only imitate Christ when other believers are around to observe them doing it. Being perceived as spiritual is all that matters. Jesus addressed this in Matthew 6:5–6 (CSB):

> *Whenever you pray, you must not be like the hypocrites, because they love to pray standing in the synagogues and on the street corners to be seen by people. Truly I tell you, they have their reward. But when you pray, go into your private room, shut your door, and pray to your Father who is in secret. And your Father who sees in secret will reward you.*

Why are we instructed to pray in secret? Jesus points out that the motive behind our worship is what determines if we are committed or not. The hypocrites He was referencing in this passage had no concern over worshipping God. Their concern was being seen. They wanted people to be impressed with how spiritual they were and to be thought of as committed. Weekend church services have become theaters where many people go to act.

You feel no remorse for sin. Committed relationships naturally lead to repentance. When you care for someone, you are mindful of the things that offend them. When you inevitably wrong that person, you will feel a sense of remorse over your actions and seek forgiveness. This is one of the ways the indwelling Holy Spirit guides us.

> *I say, then, walk by the Spirit and you will certainly not carry out the desire of the flesh. For the flesh desires what is against the Spirit, and the Spirit desires what is against the flesh; these are opposed to each other, so that you don't do what you want. But if you are led by the Spirit, you are not under the law.* (**Galatians 5:16–18**), **CSB**.

Paul tells us in this passage that the Holy Spirit is essential in our lives if we are to live for God; we cannot do it on our own. It is when the Spirit speaks to us that we can see the sin, or the desires of the flesh, in our lives. Without the guidance of the Holy Spirit, we fall victim to our sin and do things that are contrary to the image of a committed Christian. When we fall short of God's standard, it is the Holy Spirit that makes it known. This insight should result in remorse. We should grieve the unrepented sin in our lives and praise God when He forgives us. Anyone who claims to be Christian yet feels no guilt over sin is not committed. Christians who turn their backs on God and assume their relationships are fine, are merely involved.

Hebrews 3:8 tells us not to *"harden our hearts."* This is the result of unrepentant sin. You cannot grow in a relationship with Christ if you allow sin to build up. It creates distance from God. We cannot clearly hear from the Holy Spirit when sin stands in the way.

You do not desire to grow in your relationship with God. Every committed relationship grows. Growth, however, does not happen by accident; it takes effort and time. No matter how great a marriage is, a spouse should always want it to become better. This is how we should view our relationship with God. Our love for Christ can always grow to something more. Involved Christians are lazy. Committed Christians desire a growing relationship with Christ and put in the work.

LEAVE IT BEHIND

The Apostle Paul gave us a great definition of what a committed Christian is to look like.

> *Therefore, I say this and testify in the Lord: You should no longer walk as the Gentiles do, in the futility of their thoughts. They are darkened in their understanding, excluded from the life of God, because of the ignorance that is in them and because of the hardness of their hearts. They became callous and gave themselves over to promiscuity for the practice of every kind of impurity with a desire for more and more. But that is not how you came to know Christ, assuming you heard about him and were taught by him, as the truth is in Jesus, to take off your former way of life, the old self that is corrupted by deceitful desires, to be renewed in the spirit of your minds, and to put on the new self, the one created according to God's likeness in righteousness and purity of the truth.* (**Ephesians 4:17–24**), **CSB**.

Paul wrote this epistle to the Christians living in Ephesus. In its time, the city was beautiful and wealthy but full of Gentiles who committed horrible acts. Pagan worship was prominent, and all kinds of unthinkable sins were practiced.

Many of the Christians in Ephesus participated in these sinful acts before they came to know Christ. Unfortunately, some of the believers had reverted to their former ways. Paul used this letter to reiterate the image of a committed Christian. We are to leave our former ways

REDEFINITION | *Matthew Clark*

of life behind. We are not supposed to act as we did before. Change is one of the most evident characteristics of Christianity.

The first year of my marriage was very difficult. My wife would agree. In college, I lived in a townhome with five of my best friends. We watched movies, played video games, and watched college football. That was all we did. It was amazing. However, when I got married after college, I initially thought I could continue living that lifestyle free of responsibility. I quickly learned that I was wrong. Leaving my former life behind meant acting differently. It meant different priorities. It meant I no longer lived for myself but for my wife.

Scripture tells us that we are born with a sinful nature. At some point in every person's life, they will choose to sin. This sin causes separation from God, putting us in need of a savior. The sacrifice of Jesus Christ on the cross makes available to us this salvation we desperately need. It frees us from the bondage of sin, returning us to the spiritual state that God originally intended. There is no greater gift known to man than that of Jesus Christ.

However, while we are spiritually delivered from the penalty of sin, we still live with our sinful nature that we were born with. This nature, passed down from Adam, is what causes Christians to pull away from God. Paul tells us, in the passage above, to resist this pull. Every Christian is to seek God daily in an attempt to conquer this sinful nature that still infects us. We are to imitate Christ and turn from our old ways.

When a person commits to Jesus, there should be a noticeable change. It is the difference between being broken and fixed. Salvation repairs us spiritually in the eyes of God. Many people claim a relationship with Christ with no observable difference. When a person professes Christianity, yet continues to live as their old self, they are committing Identity Theft. Scripture tells us that *"if anyone is in Christ, he is a new creation; the old has passed away, and see, the new has come"*

(2 Corinthians 5:17, CSB). Involved Christians continue to walk in the flesh. Committed Christians walk in the Spirit.

GET IN THE WHEELBARROW

What does it truly mean to believe in something? I believe the roof of my house will not cave in. I also believe in myself to resist any temptation that comes my way. What is the difference between the two? While these two statements both use the word "believe," I live out the faith I have in my roof more than the faith I have in myself. My actions prove my belief.

The way you can tell I trust my roof is that I sleep in my house every night. I trust it so much that I am comfortable with my wife and children being there also. I do not have the same faith in myself. I hope I resist every temptation that comes my way, but I am not going to put myself in a situation where I may fail. I do not fully believe in myself. I am a person with a sinful nature which means I am flawed and can fall to sin if I am not careful. While I am confident that I would overcome, I am not willing to fully place my trust in my abilities like I trust my roof. I am going to put up guardrails that will limit the number of temptations I face. Our actions show the difference between "believing" and "believing in" something.

There is an old story about a man who set up a tightrope across the Grand Canyon. He pulled together a crowd that wanted to see if he could successfully walk across the rope without falling off, which would have likely resulted in his death. He asked the crowd if there was anyone there who believed he could walk across. Not a single hand went up. No one believed in him.

He stepped out onto the rope and successfully walked across, and back, to the amazement of everyone watching. He was greeted with cheers and applause. He was not done yet. He then asked the crowd if anyone there believed he could walk across the rope while pushing a wheelbarrow at the same time. Only a couple of hands went up. Walking across by yourself is one thing but pushing a wheelbarrow on a narrow rope is entirely different. Rising to the challenge, the man pushed the wheelbarrow all the way across and back again.

The crowd was out of control. Was there anything this man could not do? He asked one more question to the crowd as he prepared for his final act: "Does anyone here think that I can push this wheelbarrow across with a person inside?" At this point, everyone in the crowd was a believer. Every hand went up in faith that this man could do what he said. Looking at the crowd, he then asked for a volunteer. Not a single hand went up.

This story perfectly illustrates what it means to believe in something. It takes nothing to think a man can push a wheelbarrow across the Grand Canyon. Actually getting in the wheelbarrow, however, takes everything. You are putting your life on the line. You are invested. If the man pushing the wheelbarrow loses his balance, you are going over the edge with him. You will both perish.

This is what God wants from you: everything. He wants you to put all of your trust in Him. No matter how terrifying it is to walk the tightrope of life, you can trust that God will never let you fall. At times, it will be terrifying. There will be moments that do not make sense. Making Him your Lord means giving Him everything. You go where He wants you to go. It is taking the knowledge you have and putting it into action.

God does not care if you think He exists. He does not care if you think Jesus came back from the dead. It is what you do with that knowledge that matters to God. If salvation hinged on the word "believe," simply meaning knowledge, that would make the Devil the world's greatest Christian. Think about it. More than anyone, Satan knows the implications of what happened on the cross. He was there. James 2:29 says, *"You believe that God is one. Good! Even the demons believe—and they shudder."* Even with the knowledge they possess, they still choose to turn away from God.

Knowledge is only the beginning. Becoming fully dependent on God means trusting Him completely. With our lives. Our finances. Our families. It is interesting to think of the world's definition of maturity. A person is considered mature when they can live life on their own; when they are fully independent. They no longer need Mom and Dad to make their decisions or to pay their bills. They make their own choices.

This is not the case with Christianity. It is the opposite. As we grow in our spiritual maturity, we become more dependent on Christ. We avoid being independent of Him. Being committed means seeking God in everything we do. Committing to God means we stop committing identity theft and start living lives that submit to the Spirit.

TAKE ACTION

Make a list of ways you can show your commitment to God. After making that list, see if any of those actions can be done for your own glorification instead of the Lord's. Is there anything on your list that you want people to see you doing? What is the motive behind each action?

IN REVIEW

1. How a person defines "believe" is the difference between being saved or not.

2. The great deception is that there are Christians who do not even know they are committing identity theft.

3. People have been tricked into thinking they are spiritually secure.

4. Nowhere in Scripture are we told to live out our faith in particular time blocks.

5. The motive behind our worship is what determines if we are committed or not.

6. Committed relationships naturally lead to repentance.

7. Growth, in a relationship, does not happen by accident.

8. When a person commits to Jesus, there should be a noticeable change.

9. Believing in Jesus takes the knowledge we have and puts it into action.

10. As we grow in our spiritual maturity, we become more dependent on Christ.

Unarmed Soldiers

reDefined: Sin

"You contribute nothing to your salvation except the sin that made it necessary."

Jonathan Edwards

Do not be conformed to this age, but be transformed by the renewing of your mind, so that you may discern what is the good, pleasing, and perfect will of God. (**Romans 12:2**), **CSB**.

MEET THE VILLAIN

Before the start of WWII, the allied nations made the controversial decision of appeasing Nazi Germany in the hopes of avoiding another conflict. Many would agree that hindsight now proves it was the wrong decision. This appeasement led to the increased confidence and military strength of Germany. Neville Chamberlain, the Prime Minister of Great Britain, championed the peace talks and was instrumental in the Munich Agreement (the settlement reached by Germany, Great Britain, France, and Italy).

There was debate over whether or not appeasement was the correct move. Was it wrong to avoid a conflict with Germany? Many saw the British Prime Minister as weak over his eagerness for peace. It is hard to blame him. He once said, "When I think of those four terrible years [WWI], and I think of the 7 million young men who were killed, the 13 million who were wounded, I feel it was my duty to strain every nerve to avoid a repetition of the first world war."

Chamberlain desperately wanted peace and thought Hitler was like-minded. We now see he was wrong about the German leader. Some argue that it should have been obvious. Hitler outlined many of his ideas in *Mein Kampf*, his 1925 autobiographical manifesto that expressed his plans for Germany. He did not hide his disgust for the Jews and other neighboring nations. It eventually became apparent that Germany needed to be stopped, and after three years of appeasement, Neville Chamberlain stepped down as Prime Minister. Winston Churchill took his place. The world was once again at war.

It is easy to read about this and fault Chamberlain for being indecisive. He did not see Hitler for who he really was. Chamberlain saw Hitler as someone who could be reasoned with and not the villain he is known as today. The sad truth is that many Christians have made the same mistake of appeasing the enemy. The Church has redefined and minimized who we are at war with. The enemy, in this case, is Satan.

Every story has a villain. The hero, or protagonist, faces someone or something that is trying to prevent them from succeeding. God's story is no different. We are up against an antagonist who aggressively preys on us. His only desire is to create distance between humanity and its Creator.

The Bible says very little about how Satan came to be. Isaiah 14:12 appears to show that he was once an angel that wanted to *"make himself like the most high."* His desire to sit above God resulted in his eviction from heaven. Since then, God has allowed him to temporarily be the ruler of this world (John 12:31) and he will do anything in his power to stand against God and all His followers.

Satan's disdain for God is called sin, and it is implanted in every human walking the earth. The result of the Fall (Genesis 3) is that we are all born with a sinful nature leading us to choose ourselves over God (Romans 5:18). Everything we desire is in opposition to the Lord. Sin is the reason humanity needs salvation.

All believers should have an accurate view of the devastating effects of sin: It brings death. It causes separation from God (Isaiah 59:2). Sin is an enemy that will never stop fighting against us as long as we live in these corrupted bodies with these sinful natures. Sadly, most Christians have a small view of sin. It is something we keep to ourselves, something we do not talk about. We have been convinced sin is no big deal, that sin is something we should overlook.

I am amazed at how little this enemy is preached about from the pulpit. The power of sin over a person should be a topic that is discussed frequently, not avoided. We must see sin for what it really is. We must realize how powerful it can be in our lives if we are not on guard. The enemy is always at our doorstep, and like the British Prime Minister with Hitler, many Christians seek appeasement and not war. We must stop underestimating our greatest enemy in battle. This fight will not end until Jesus returns. Why have we forgotten this? The Devil has not. As General James Mattis once said, "No war is over until the enemy says it's over. We may think it over, we may declare it over, but in fact, the enemy gets a vote." In light of this, we should have an extremely high view of sin. We must never underestimate its influence.

If we are to win this battle, we must first correctly identify the enemy. We are only telling half the story when we label the Devil as the only villain. He is not alone in his opposition to God. Whatever sin corrupts, or infects, is made into an adversary of God. It is easy to think that this enemy is far away. In actuality, this enemy is very close to us. Greg

Koukl makes this point in his book *The Story of Reality*:

> We are not the victims. We are the victimizers. The evil in the world is not out there. It is in us. Put simply, we are guilty, and we know it.[10]

Here is the good news: Before giving your life to Christ, you were on the wrong side of the war. You were fighting for the losing team. However, after turning to Jesus and making Him your Lord, you no longer battle with God. You have defected to the winning side. What many overlook is that the enemy is still close by. Your soul may have been saved, but your sinful nature remains at war with God.

Your sinful nature will urge you to break ranks and fight once again for your old leader. It will try to convince you that you are more important than God, that what you want is all that matters. The Devil uses this corrupted part of us to speak lies and to deceive. We are fighting against an enemy that is both outside and inside of us.

ARM YOURSELF

The impact of the enemy has been felt since the beginning of time. God breathed life into creation and concluded His week by making man in His image. The Garden of Eden showed us what perfection looks like. By breaking the guidelines that God established, Adam and Eve allowed sin to enter the world, resulting in the corruption of the entire human race. They fell short of the standard that God had set up. T. Desmond Alexander said, "From the outset of creation, God intended that the earth would become a holy garden-city in which he would dwell alongside human beings. However, the disobedience of Adam and Eve jeopardized this divine project."[11] The perfect world that God created had become corrupted with sin.

---

10 Koukl, Greg. *The Story of Reality*, p. 78.
11 Alexander, T. Desmond. *From Eden to the New Jerusalem*, p. 74.

We must see sin for what it really is. We must not diminish the impact it has on what it corrupts. Wayne Grudem defines sin as "any failure to conform to the moral law of God in act, attitude, or nature."[12] It is not just what we do, but what we say and think that can be sinful. In the Bible, sin is often defined as "missing the mark." Like an archer's arrow hitting outside the bullseye. Millard Erickson tells us that:

> Sin is always sin against God, since it is failure to hit the mark which he has set, his standard. This mark that is missed is perfect love to God and perfect obedience to Him. We miss the mark and sin against God when, for example, we fail to love our brother, since love of brother would inevitably follow if we truly loved God. Similarly, sinning against one's own body is mistreatment of God's temple (1 Cor. 3:16–17) and therefore a sin against God.[13]

God's standard is revealed in Scripture. Reading and knowing the Bible defines what our target is for living. Missing that target is living a life outside of God's desire for us. Sin comes in the form of other targets, causing us to aim at things that are not God. This is the reason I pity unbelievers who are slaves to sin. They think the targets they hit bring fulfillment, purpose, and value. Targets such as lust, anger, envy, and every other sin. This is far from the truth. Without Jesus, they have no choice but to hit outside the mark.

What does this mean for the Christian? A believer can still "miss the mark" or fail to live up to the standard that God has put in place. It would be foolish to say that sin no longer has an impact on someone who is saved simply because they are covered by the blood of Christ. While sin cannot affect our standing with God, it can still have an impact on our fellowship with Him. It can make us live outside the abundant life that God wants for us. Giving yourself to Christ does not mean that the enemy leaves you alone. In fact, I believe it is the opposite. How much effort do you think the Devil gives to those he is not worried about?

---

12 Grudem, Wayne. *Systematic Theology*, p. 490.
13 Erickson, Millard J. *Christian Theology*, p. 569.

Imagine you are fighting in a war. You are sitting in a field with your weapon ready for an imminent attack. Looking out, you see two enemy soldiers running your way. You prepare yourself for battle. As the two soldiers get closer, you realize only one of them is armed; the other does not have a weapon. You now have a decision to make: which soldier will you shoot first?

I imagine most people would make the same choice and fire upon the man carrying the weapon. Why? The answer is simple: only one of the soldiers poses a threat. The unarmed soldier does not appear to be dangerous.

Unfortunately, the American Church is full of unarmed soldiers. Full of people that the Devil overlooks because he does not fear them. Full of people that are not worth the effort of attacking. These statements sound harsh, but they are true. We must arm ourselves.

We do this by seeking God and resisting sin. You are more of a threat to the Devil when you are closer to the Lord. The Devil hates it when believers hit the mark. He hates it when we are making an impact for the Kingdom like an armed soldier on the battlefield. Armed Christians are the ones whom the Devil is going to go after more. He knows he cannot steal you away from God, but do you realize he is perfectly capable of stealing your impact as a Christian? A soldier with no weapon is not a risk; why would the Devil waste his time?

Christians arm themselves when they commit to a daily quiet time with Scripture and prayer. When they grow in fellowship with other believers. When they worship God with their lifestyles. When they share the Gospel with those who are spiritually dead.

Ask yourself this question: Which soldier are you? Are you armed and ready for battle or are you a soldier who continually forgets his gun? If you are armed, be ready for the ambush. As you grow closer to the Lord, be ready for opposition. God desires us to be soldiers that run into battle, not retreat.

If you are not facing any hardship, it may mean you are not a threat to the Devil. If you are arming yourself, know that the Devil is going to come after you with everything he has. He will not win the war, but he can win the battle if we allow him.

I can think of many pastors who have lost their influence because they flirted with sin. A man that I have followed closely for years was recently caught in sexual immorality. He published material and did seminars that positively impacted the faith of millions of believers. The Devil came after him with everything he had and succeeded. This man's organization is now changing its name, radio stations have dropped his broadcast, and what was once a reputable ministry, is now marred by scandal.

We should never fear the Devil. Even under attack, we can resist him with the power of the Holy Spirit living inside us. But we must always be on guard and ready for what may come. Think of what could happen to your testimony, your spiritual journey, if you fall victim to sin. Non-believers are watching and if they see us being controlled by the enemy, the impact could be dire. The Devil wins many battles this way.

This is why a low view of sin is destructive to evangelism. Many believers within the Church are falling to the attacks of the Devil. Starting off on fire for God, they begin losing battles to the enemy, causing them to lower their weapons. Once this happens, the Devil has taken away their impact.

OPEN FIRE

It is very easy to see sin in someone else while ignoring your own struggles. Why do we forget that we cannot keep secrets from God? He knows exactly what we are dealing with. He knows what is holding us back from growing closer to Him, yet we act as if we can keep it to ourselves. This is a trick of the Devil. Sin has more control over someone when it is kept private. This is why James 5:16 says, "Therefore, confess your sins to one another and pray for one another, so that you may be healed."

When sin is brought to light, confession happens. Practically speaking, the best way to defeat sin is to find an accountability partner who can check on your progress. Accountability is a guardrail that helps you stay focused, and it only occurs when confession happens. Accountability partners must know what you are struggling with.

I see the opposite happening within the Church. Instead of exposing our sins and bringing them to light, we tighten our grip. We harbor and nurture them. In reality, sin is running rampant within the Church and if we are going to make progress on the culture for Christ, we have to first address this issue. How do we expect the world to turn from their sin when we cannot turn from our own? How can we tell someone not to lust when a majority of Christian men are addicted to pornography? How can we preach unity when gossip and slander are littered throughout the Church? I have seen so much hate and disdain on Sunday mornings during a worship service. We must stop harboring our sin.

After identifying the villain and arming ourselves, the next step is to open fire. It is not enough that we see the sin in our lives; we have to see it the way God does. Having a high view of sin means it is impossible to cater to it any longer. It means going to war.

When we allow sin to live in our lives, it grows into more sin. It replicates. And when new sin enters in, you begin to rationalize away the impact it has on your life. *"Well, maybe it is not that bad. At least I am not as bad as such and such over there."*

My friend once illustrated sin by comparing it to a little monster that was biting at his heels. The little monster does not pose a threat in its current condition. However, that changes if you feed it. You see no big deal giving it a little food now and then. What happens, though, when you keep feeding it? Before you realize what is happening, the monster has grown in size and is now bigger than you. It now has power and authority over you. You cannot control it. This is what sin does.

When you give your life to Christ, the indwelling Holy Spirit gives you the power needed to conquer any sin. This does not mean that sin goes away; it just means you have to stay diligent and starve the monster. When you continue to feed it and let it grow, the sin that you once thought so little of, it is now a monster that you cannot control. Always view sin as a hungry enemy that wants you to feed it. No matter how small or enticing it appears, starve it.

UNDERCOVER SIN

The Praying Mantis is one of the world's most interesting creatures. There are so many fun facts about them: They eat only live food, they are the only insects that can turn their heads from side to side, they have spikes on their legs to help pin down their prey, and they are masters of disguise. They can camouflage themselves into the environment around them. They can make themselves look like leaves, sticks, and branches. It has also been discovered that they can become black at the end of the dry season to blend in with the scorched earth from the wildfires. The undetected Praying Mantis normally eats very well.

The Praying Mantis and sin operate in the same way. Sin blends in and is difficult to detect if you are not on your guard. The Devil knows this. This is the tactic he uses within the Church. I often say that the Devil does not care if he gets the credit for your fall immediately. Sin is often a slow burn and can hide for some time being undetectable to the believer. The Devil is patient.

1 Peter 5:8 warns us by saying, *"Be alert and of sober mind. Your enemy the Devil prowls around like a roaring lion looking for someone to devour."*

Why do we not heed this warning? I had a friend once tell me about a time when he was in Africa on a mission trip. He was part of a group that was traveling from village to village telling Africans about Jesus. One time, a lady approached and asked my friend to come to her house to pray for her little son who was sick. My friend agreed and followed her, leaving his group behind.

He arrived at a small hut where the lady and her family lived. My friend walked in, saw the sick little boy, and prayed for him. After staying for a short time, my friend heard yelling outside that sounded familiar, it was his travel guide. My friend had not informed the guide he was going to the house, and the guide was in a panic. He told my friend that he must never wander away unsupervised again. When he asked why, the guide responded with one word: "lions." That whole time he was in danger of being attacked by a lion and did not even realize it.

The Church must open its eyes regarding sin. We must become better at recognizing when the Devil is trying to devour us. We must train ourselves to see when sin is gaining a stronghold in our lives. Like being in the African wilderness, we are in danger of being devoured by a predator that is out to get us. Let us discuss some of the sins that the Church is overlooking, some of the sins that are undercover.

The Sin of "Busy." The world has never before benefited from technology like it does today. A handwritten letter used to take days to get to its destination; now an email can be delivered to the other side of the world in seconds. If someone wanted to travel from England to the United States, they would sail in a boat across the Atlantic under difficult conditions. Today, there are talks of people soon being able to travel to the moon commercially. Technology has made everything easier and faster.

American culture is always on the move. Everyone is always busy. Sports, dance recitals, work, etc. Nobody has extra time anymore. Every hour is accounted for. Sadly, spirituality has suffered the most from this phenomenon. Not only has church attendance lost its importance, but spiritual disciplines (scripture reading, prayer, fasting, worship, and serving) are being ignored. I can agree that technology has provided multiple benefits to Christianity and the Church, but we have to admit that the fast-paced mindset has done significant damage to many Christians. Pastor Adrian Rogers once said, "If Satan can't make you bad, he'll make you busy."

Is busyness keeping you from living for the Lord? Are you giving in to the tempting thoughts of pushing off spirituality for other things? We have to fight against this. Our sinful natures will try and rationalize our spiritual procrastination by giving priority to other things over God:

"I can read my Bible later. I have to finish _____ first."

"I have to miss Church this week to get _____ done. I'll just go next week."

Remember that part of the enemy still lives inside us and is trying to put distance between you and God.

Kris Lundgaard puts it like this:

> Indwelling sin takes advantage of our natural laziness and negligence in spiritual things, enticing us to lay aside spiritual duties one by one. It won't at first get God completely out of our minds. But it will talk us into thinking of him less and less, making us think we can get by with a little less prayer, shorter or fewer private devotions—until he, at last, convinces us that we can get along without talking to God at all.[14]

The Sin of "Religion." In the last couple of years, I figured out that I am more productive when I have a checklist. I cannot stand the sight of empty checkboxes next to my to-do list. It inspires me to complete

14 Lundgaard, Kris. *The Enemy Within*, p. 116.

my tasks. I believe Christians can become the same way when it comes to their faith. This is what happens when faith becomes religion; religion is about completing tasks. It is about checking off the list. Did I pray today? Did I go to church this week? Did I do my bible study?

These are spiritual disciplines that every Christian should be doing. The thing to consider is the motive. Why are we supposed to do these things? We do them to grow closer to God, plain and simple. Unfortunately, many Christians are doing them to check off their list. Going through the motions of religion takes away the spiritual benefits of the action.

This is why Jesus had so many harsh words for the Pharisees. They were a group of people who were literally following all the commands of Scripture yet falling short in the eyes of God. You see, Jesus is more concerned with the heart behind the action. It matters why we do the things we do. If our hearts are not in the right place, it becomes sin because it is not done for the glory of God.

Checklists make you feel good about yourself. They make you feel accomplished. Tim Keller is correct when he says, "This means that you can rebel against God and be alienated from Him either by breaking his rules or by keeping them all diligently."[15] We have to avoid becoming American Pharisees: Christians who make Christianity all about themselves.

The Sin of "Stagnation." Do not fall victim to the idea that salvation is all that matters. It is merely the beginning of the journey. We miss so much of who Jesus is when we become Christians and do nothing with our faith. It is common for men to aggressively pursue the woman they want to marry. They take them on dates. They buy them jewelry. Then, after they get married, they quit doing those things. They think, "I'm married. I got the girl. There is no need to pursue her anymore." It is tragic when this happens to a wife but more tragic when it happens to God.

15 Keller, Tim. *The Prodigal God*, p. 42.

Apathy is defined as a "lack of interest, enthusiasm, or concern." This word should never be used to describe Christians but, sadly, is. It is a sin to be stagnant in faith. It saddens God when He sees the Church having little interest in knowing Him more.

This is the reason stagnation is a sin: It makes us neutral. It prevents growth. It hinders passion. Think of what happens to water when it becomes stagnant. Mold and bacteria can grow, making it a breeding ground for insects that carry disease. Mice, rats, and all kinds of vermin are on the hunt for watering holes. This is why people are advised to get rid of stagnant water near their homes in hopes of avoiding these negative effects.

It is similar with our faith. If we become stagnant, we run the risk of becoming a place where sin grows. Sin is a disease that spreads in stagnant Christians.

BLENDING IN

Sin has been allowed to reside within the Church for too long. We have cozied up and fed it causing it to grow. Think of what this does to the image of the Church. Hypocrisy has become a common descriptor of Christianity because it is true. So many people within the Church do not look any different from those outside the Church. Two things that made the early Church stand out were that it lived counter-culturally, and it attempted to eradicate sin from within.

We are called to live differently from the culture around us. Why? Because the world is enslaved to sin. We are not supposed to do something simply because that is how everyone else does it. We are supposed to parent differently, use our time differently, and treat others differently. Remember that Jesus never blended in; He stood out.

This is why addressing sin within the Church needs to become a top priority again. I say again because it used to be. Churches used to see sin as detrimental to the Christian image. This does not appear to be the case anymore. We brush it off. We do not confront other believers who are harboring their sin (I will discuss this more in chapter 6). This tolerance of sin has caused many Churches to blend in with the culture, making them invisible. Making them just like everyone else.

It is foolish to think that we will fully eliminate sin within the Church. This will only happen when Jesus comes. But this should not discourage us from giving everything we have to defeating this enemy. To be clear, it will take everything we have and more. We cannot do it on our own.

When we have a high view of sin, seeing it for what it truly is, it will cause us to have a higher view of God. It leads us to the realization that we can only overcome sin with the power and help of the Holy Spirit. It is an enemy we cannot defeat with sheer determination. Francis Schaeffer once said:

> It is not we who overcome the world in our own strength. We do not have a power plant inside ourselves that can overcome the world. The overcoming is the work of the Lord Jesus Christ, as we have already seen. There can be a victory, a practical victory, if we raise the empty hands of faith moment by moment and accept the gift. "This is the victory that overcometh the world." God has promised, and the Bible has said, that there is a way to escape temptation. By God's grace, we should want that escape.[16]

The ironic thing about sin is that it reminds us of how dependent we are on the Lord. If we were able to overcome every sin and temptation with our own will, what need would we have for Jesus? For the indwelling Holy Spirit? As devastating as sin is, the forgiveness we receive from the Lord far outweighs the guilt. This is why we should

---

16 Schaeffer, Francis. *True Spirituality*, p. 86.

keep each other accountable. Not to condemn but to free. If we truly love someone, we should not want them in bondage to sin. We should want them to experience the full freedom that comes from salvation. Let us no longer appease the enemy that keeps us from fully living for Christ and, instead, raise up arms and go to war.

TAKE ACTION

Find an accountability partner. It may be beneficial to find someone older than you. Older Christians have seen and experienced things that can bring great insight. If you are able, try to meet once a week either in person or by phone. Your accountability partner should encourage you to maintain a consistent quiet time and give you the opportunity to confess any sins you may be struggling with.

IN REVIEW

1. The Church has redefined and minimized who we are at war with.

2. The power of sin over a person should be a topic that is discussed frequently, not avoided.

3. If we are to win this battle, we must first correctly identify the enemy.

4. Are you armed and ready for battle or are you a soldier who continually forgets his gun?

5. Instead of exposing our sins and bringing them to light, we tighten our grip.

6. Always view sin as a hungry monster that wants you to feed it.

7. Our sinful natures will try and rationalize our spiritual procrastination by giving priority to other things over God.

8. We have to avoid becoming American Pharisees: Christians who make Christianity all about themselves.

9. If we become stagnant, we run the risk of becoming a place where sin grows.

10. The tolerance of sin has caused many Churches to blend in with the culture, making them invisible. Making them just like everyone else.

Is He Worth It?

reDefined: Worship

*"Don't let your happiness depend on
something you may lose."*

C.S. Lewis

*Therefore, brothers and sisters, in view of the mercies of
God, I urge you to present your bodies as a living sacrifice,
holy and pleasing to God; this is your true worship.*
(**Romans 12:1**), **CSB**.

HER BEST WASN'T ENOUGH

For over 100 years, the painting Ecce Homo (Behold the man) by
Elias Garcia has been hanging in the Sanctuary of Mercy Church near
Zaragoza. It is a beautiful portrait of Jesus Christ. Due to exposure
to moisture over many years, the painting started showing signs of
deterioration. In hopes of restoring the picture, an eighty-year-old
parishioner took it upon herself to restore the mural by painting
over the worn-out areas. Her attempt at fixing the painting made the
news worldwide.

While the woman may have had good intentions, her effort resulted in making Jesus look like a "crayon sketch of a very hairy monkey in an ill-fitting tunic," as described by a BBC Europe correspondent. What was once a picture that was the source of pride for the local people was now a disfigured image of our Savior. As much as she wanted to, she was not able to restore the painting.

One of my favorite attributes of God is that He is the master of restoration. Unlike this woman, God can fully restore any person, no matter how spiritually disfigured or messed up they are. It does not matter what is in your past; God can restore you. It does not matter how many times you have sinned; God can restore you. This is what happens when we give our lives to Christ and make Him our Lord. What an amazing thing. This should cause us to give God the praise He deserves daily. It should cause us to live our lives on mission for Him. It should cause us to worship.

Worship is generally thought of as an act performed solely by religious people. The reality is that everyone worships. Christians and non-believers are alike in the fact that they give their attention and affection to something. It is how God created us. It is what we were made to do. David Foster Wallace says, "There is no such thing as not worshipping. Everybody worships. The only choice we get is what to worship."

The Devil knows that he cannot stop us from worshipping, and he has no intention to. He loves when we worship, as long as it is not Jesus. He desires to change the object of our affections, for us to worship things other than God. This is the great deception within the American Church. Many of us have been deceived into thinking that our acts of worship are bringing glory to God when, in fact, our worship is given away to other things.

I am burdened by the fact that so many Christians believe their acts of worship are giving God the honor He is due. God is the one who determines how He is worshipped, not us. Can we worship incorrectly?

Absolutely. The Bible is full of examples of unacceptable worship: When Cain's offering was rejected by God (Genesis 4:3–5). When Saul assumed the role of priest and offered the sacrifice himself (1 Samuel 13:8–14). How the believer is to find reconciliation with their brother before offering a gift to God at the altar (Matthew 5:24).

I often recommend *The Five Love Languages* by Gary Chapman to married couples. The premise of the book is that people express and experience love in five ways: words of affirmation, quality time, giving gifts, acts of service, and physical touch. Chapman calls these five expressions "love languages" and claims that different people with different personalities express and feel love in different ways. Every spouse should strive to find which love language their partner yearns for and attempt to show them love in that way. This is when they truly feel loved. It is possible, and very common, for spouses to show love the wrong way.

It is no different with our Lord. We serve a God who desires to be worshipped, but He must be worshipped correctly. This is not to say that God can only be worshipped with one specific practice; there are infinite ways to bring God glory. The sole purpose of Godly worship though, is that He is the one getting the glory. This is the trap we have fallen into. Things labeled "godly worship" are instead giving glory to something else other than God. John MacArthur has some strong words for modern churches today:

> We have many activities and little worship. We are big on ministry and small on adoration. We are disastrously pragmatic. All we want to know about is what works. We want formulas and gimmicks, and somehow in the process, we leave out that to which God has called us.[17]

How did we get here? So many churches are doing things they deem worship but, in reality, are acts that only bring glory to themselves. Is it any wonder that worship music is the most divisive aspect of churches

---

17 MacArthur, John. *Worship*, p. 51.

today? When singing to God is all about your personal preference of style, why wouldn't you be disappointed when the worship band does a song that is not on your playlist? Our church services have become a check-off list of religious activities.

An action without affection for God means nothing. So many Christians in the United States have fooled themselves into thinking God is pleased with what they are offering Him. They are deceived.

The word "worship" has been redefined to mean "any act done during a church service." A better, more biblical, definition is: "The full-life response to who God is and what He has done." Worship is what we do with the truth we know. When we fully see the truth of the Gospel, it becomes difficult to only worship God on the weekends. Worship then becomes a major part of who we are.

Ultimately, the question we need to ask ourselves is, Is God worth it? True worship happens when you honestly answer yes to that question. If you believe God is truly worth it, your life will reflect it. Your actions will reflect it.

A LIFESTYLE OF WORSHIP

I grew up playing a lot of football with my friends in the backyard. We thought we were the best players to ever step on a field. When we started high school, one of my friends suggested that we try out for the football team. We were all convinced that we would be starters and win championships.

To try out for the team, you first had to attend one of the mandatory meetings with the head coach. After going to the meeting, I quickly realized that high school football was not for me. The reason— practice was every day after school from 3:00 p.m.–7:00 p.m. No part of me wanted to stay at school any longer than I needed to. Why in the world would I choose to stay there when I could go home and watch television? I informed my friends of my decision and, sadly, any dream of winning a championship ended that day.

What made me quit was that I knew I could not give the coach what he was asking for. The coach wanted commitment. He wanted football to be all we thought about that fall semester. Imagine the reaction I would have received from the coach if I had asked to only practice once a week and still play on the team Friday nights. I did not love the game enough to give that much of myself.

Does this not sound an awful lot like Christians? We want to be on the team. We want to experience winning. However, we are not willing to give ourselves fully. It is like we have accepted a full-time job and are only showing up to work twenty hours a week.

God is not interested in part-time Christians. He does not even want us to clock out. If you have given your life to Jesus and made Him your Lord, the expectation is that your entire lifestyle reflects Christ. God expects to have all of you.

Imagine if I approached my wife and said, "I promise to be your husband only twenty percent of the time." Is that a marriage she would be interested in? We need to get out of the mindset that our worship of God is something that we can just turn off. That worship is something that only happens on Sundays at church.

This means that we need to guard our every thought. What we allow in our minds affects our worship. How we feel about people affects our worship. Look at Matthew 5:23–24: *"So if you are offering your gift on the altar, and there you remember that your brother or sister has something against you, leave your gift there in front of the altar. First go and be reconciled with your brother or sister, and then come and offer your gift."*

In this passage, Jesus is telling His listeners that HOW we approach God matters. When there is a relationship in need of reconciliation or there is someone you need to forgive, that is a part of your life that God does not just overlook. You cannot worship God with the same mouth you curse your brother or sister with.

I remember a time when I was the Kids Pastor at my church and I overheard a couple of boys saying some pretty negative things about my daughter. They had a run-in earlier, and my daughter did not respond kindly. These boys began calling her names behind her back and saying some bad things.

I approached these fourth graders and told them I overheard what they were saying. It was hilarious listening to these kids try and get out of trouble. They began telling me how much they enjoyed my message that morning and how funny they thought I was. I ended the conversation by saying, "Guys, I appreciate what you are saying, but she's still my daughter. You need to go and make things right." To their credit, they did.

This is what God sees when we approach Him with an act of worship. We go before Him and say all the nice words we can think of. We raise our hands in worship surrendering everything to God. The truth is, most of us are not surrendering everything. We are holding on to grudges. We are living in sin. If God were only concerned with the moment, no matter what our lives looked like, that act of worship would be enough. But God sees our entire life as an act of worship. We cannot say "yes" to God on Sundays but "no" to Him every other day. True worship is the way we strive to make every aspect of our lifestyle pleasing to Him and also seeking repentance when we sin.

WORSHIP BRINGS FOCUS

In his book *Worship Matters*, Bob Kauflin writes about the sin of idolatry. He says:

> Whenever we love and serve anything in place of God, we're engaging in idolatry. We love our idols because we think they'll provide the joy that comes from God alone. We think having them will truly satisfy us. We think they're worthy of our worship. Of course, we're wrong.[18]

Most believers would not think they struggle with idolatry. We tend to think idolatry only happens in movies like *Indiana Jones and the Temple of Doom*. While we are not pulling out people's hearts and offering them to fake gods, this is a sin that many Christians do not even realize they are dealing with. In fact, I will be bold enough to say that idolatry is happening in most of our American churches today.

We are finding our hope in things other than God. Charles Spurgeon once said, "Whatever is your greatest joy and treasure, that is your god." Anytime our focus leaves the Lord, and we give glory to something else, we are committing idolatry.

I began leading worship services when I was fifteen years old. I will admit that so many times my focus was not on God during worship; it was on me. The view of myself had become my idol. Have you raised your hands during worship hoping that people would see you do it? Is your church attendance based on the idea that you want people to know you are a regular attender? What is your reason for posting pictures of your morning bible study on social media? Is it to encourage people to have a quiet time, or do you simply want people to comment on how godly you are?

We have made ourselves into idols and do not even see it. I believe this happens mostly because we forget what God has done for us. Call it spiritual amnesia. When our eyes are open to the truth of what Jesus did for us on the cross, and we remind ourselves of that truth daily, we cannot not worship God (sorry for the double negative). True biblical worship happens when we have proper focus.

---

18 Kauflin, Bob. *Worship Matters*, p. 21.

I often say that the biggest group of complainers were God's chosen people: the Israelites from the book of Exodus. What makes it worse is that they had no reason to complain. Think of all the miracles and amazing things that God did through Moses. Here are a few:

1. Aaron's rod became a serpent (Exodus 7:8–13).

2. The ten plagues on Egypt (Exodus 7–12).

3. The Exodus of Israel from Egypt (Exodus 12:40–41).

4. God led them with a pillar of cloud by day and fire by night (Exodus 13:17–22).

5. God made a path through the Red Sea (Exodus 14:21–29).

6. The Egyptians were drowned in the Red Sea (Exodus 14:25–31).

7. God turned the bitter water sweet and made it drinkable (Exodus 15:22–25).

8. The Lord provided manna and quail (Exodus 16:1–21).

9. Water in the rock (Exodus 17:2–6)._

10. The battle against Amalek (Exodus 17:9-13).

These are just a few of the things the Israelites got to witness. After seeing all the wonders and miracles from God, why were they so quick to turn away from Him? It happened almost instantly. First, look at Exodus 14:30–31:

> *Thus the Lord saved Israel that day from the hand of the Egyptians, and Israel saw the Egyptians dead on the seashore. When Israel saw the great power which the Lord had used against the Egyptians, the people feared the Lord, and they believed in the Lord and in His servant Moses.*

Imagine what the Israelites were feeling at that moment. Put yourself in their shoes, or more accurately, their sandals. You remember that your people had been slaves in Egypt for four hundred and thirty years. You witnessed the power of God through Moses and were freed from your captors. After leaving Egypt, you discovered that Pharaoh had changed his mind and set out to bring you back into slavery. You approached the Red Sea and were unable to cross it until Moses used his staff to part the sea in half. You crossed safely to the other side. You then looked back and saw the Egyptian chariots beginning to cross over in pursuit. A feeling of dread came over you. You then realized that the freedom you were experiencing would soon come to an end. Suddenly, though, you see the water that was once divided come crashing down onto the Egyptians, those who sought to make you slaves again. You stand there in silence and watch the dead Egyptian bodies wash up on the shore. Your captors are no more. You are no longer slaves. What do you do at this moment? How do you respond to such a loving and powerful God?

Their initial response was correct: they feared and believed in the Lord. How could you not trust God after seeing what He had done? What they had experienced should have resulted in a lifetime of praise and worship to God. This, however, was not the case. After praising God for His works, they set out again on their journey into the wilderness. Three days later though, they were without water (Exodus 15:22–27). They complained, yet God provided. The most shocking part of this story comes in Exodus 16:2–3 when the Israelites were without food:

> The whole congregation of the sons of Israel grumbled against Moses and Aaron in the wilderness. The sons of Israel said to them, "Would that we had died by the Lord's hand in the land of Egypt, when we sat by the pots of meat, when we ate bread to the full; for you have brought us out into this wilderness to kill this whole assembly with hunger."

I truly feel bad for Moses every time I read this story. In this passage, the Israelites make the most foolish claim in all of Scripture by saying that they would rather return to slavery if it meant they could go to bed every night with a full belly. They saw slavery as a better situation than the one they were currently in.

Imagine what Moses was thinking after hearing that. How could they respond this way? Did they not remember what God did for them three days earlier? The answer is no. They had forgotten. They had taken their focus off of God and put it on themselves. They were hungry. They needed to be fed. It was all that mattered at that moment. Not that God could be trusted and that He would provide. They were focused on themselves, causing them to forget the greatness of God.

Focus is really what worship is all about. Satan attempts to get us to turn our eyes away from God and onto other things. I think back to the story of Peter walking on the water with Jesus in Matthew 14. When did Peter begin to sink? It was when he took his eyes off of Christ and focused on the wind and the waves.

Christians, we are living in a time of great distraction. There are so many things out there that pull our attention away from Jesus. These distractions cause us to forget what God has done. We are being fooled into thinking that things other than Christ can bring us happiness and fulfillment. Fight the temptation to think this way.

When we willingly place our focus on God, we are showing Him that He is worth it. We are showing Him that we remember. That He is worth our time. That He is worthy of our entire lives. Donald Whitney says,

> The more we focus on God, the more we understand and appreciate His infinite worth. As we understand and appreciate this, we can't help but respond to Him. Just as an indescribable sunset or breathtaking mountaintop vista evokes a spontaneous response, so we cannot encounter the worthiness of God without the response of worship.[19]

19 Whitney, Donald. *Spiritual Disciplines for the Christian Life*, p. 104.

HOW DO WE WORSHIP?

So how do we accurately define worship in our lives? It begins by realizing that God is worth it. If you do not fully believe that God is worthy, then you will not dedicate your whole life to Him. Nobody gives everything for a cause if they are not fully on board. Remember, God is looking for full-time followers who are willing to put their lives on the line. He is looking for believers who will use everything at their disposal to give God the glory.

I am a huge fan of the James Bond films. I was a kid when I first saw 007 in action and I remember sitting in front of the television screen in awe of the gadgets he used. One of my favorite characters from the series was the inventor named Q. His job was to invent the gadgets and gizmos that helped James Bond get out of tight situations. If it was not for Q, James Bond surely would have died many movies ago.

Isn't it amazing that God equips us also? He has a plan for our lives that involves us using the gifts He has given. I have enjoyed seeing kids and students grow in their faith and figure out the talents and passions that God has given them. It pains me to see students wander from God and use their gifts on something other than bringing Him glory. In Romans 12:4–6, Paul says:

> Now as we have many parts in one body, and all the parts do not have the same function, in the same way we who are many are one body in Christ and individually members of one another. According to the grace given to us, we have different gifts...

I love this passage because it shows the unifying nature of the Church. Like a body, the church has many different parts that have different roles to play. We all contribute to the sole purpose of the entire body: to bring God the glory. So, what does that look like for you? Ask yourself this question: What am I passionate about?

I am always amazed at the diversity of passion within the church body. There are so many things that I am not passionate about. Helping in the nursery, cleaning, and paperwork (to list a few). However, some people are extremely passionate about doing those things. I knew a lady that loved doing organizational work in the office. She would come in with the biggest smile on her face because she was able to live out her passion for the Lord. I felt guilty about asking her to do office work because I hated it so much. She told me, "Matt, this frees you up to do other things for the Kingdom." She had a great perspective.

The first time I saw my current house, I fell head over heels. It was love at first sight. The funny thing is that I did not even step foot inside the house. What I loved was the property. Our house is located out in the country, so it is very green and very quiet. After spending the day moving in, I remember standing outside and looking up at the sky. The stars looked different out in the country because there were no city lights. It was beautiful. The moon was the biggest I had ever seen. What really stood out was how bright it was.

As we all know, it is not the moon that produces light. The moon merely reflects light from the sun. When we do not see the sun at night, it is the moon that reminds us the sun is still out there. This is what happens when we use our gifts and talents to bring glory to God. We are showing the world that there is a God worthy of praise. Some people will come to know Christ because you reflected the light of God with a lifestyle of worship. Do not waste the gifts and passions that God has given you on created things; use them, instead, to glorify the eternal God.

Can you imagine what would happen if every believer used their gifts to glorify God? Perhaps the trends would change. Currently, so many churches in the United States are declining in numbers. Eighty percent of all Southern Baptist churches are in decline or have plateaued. I have a guess as to why this is happening. I believe it is a lack of passion.

I think many Churches may be saying the right words but do not accompany the words with actions. Worship is when you live out what you believe. I am tired of seeing the Devil have victory over our country. He is having victory over our culture, our marriages, and our children. The only way this will change is if we live out our Christianity with a lifestyle of worship.

The final thing we can do to accurately define worship in our lives is to focus on the emptiness of our sin. I know this is a strange thing to say. Allow me to elaborate. Sin has a way of blurring our focus. When we allow ourselves to fall into sin, our fellowship with God is affected. As I said earlier, the Devil's main goal is to deceive us. He does not want us to see God accurately. He wants us to put something else in the place of Christ.

One of the hardest things about youth ministry is convincing students that sin will eventually leave them empty and void. Many students in the midst of sin do not see this. Sin for them is fun and enjoyable. This is what Satan does. He convinces you that sin is great and that it will remain that way. The reality is that 100 percent of the time, sin will eventually leave you empty. When you put your hope and trust in something of this world, it will not last. It never does—sometimes it just takes a little longer to realize it.

The emptiness of sin can be a road sign that points you to God. The emptiness of sin shows us how great God truly is. Jesus is the only thing that can eternally satisfy. He is the only thing that can bring us unending joy. He is the only thing that can fully restore you. Look back on your life and see what sins God has delivered you from. If that does not make you want to worship Him with everything in you, you do not understand the full scope of salvation.

CALL HIM FATHER

I got home from work one day to be greeted by my family. It is the best thing about being a dad and husband. When I walked through the door, I hugged my wife first and then leaned down to hug my kids. My daughter, who is my only daughter, looked up at me with a smile and said, "Hello, Matt."

It took me by surprise because I was taught that calling a parent by their first name is disrespectful. She was trying to be funny and push the boundaries, so she said it again, "Hello, Matt." Before I could respond, my wife knelt down beside her and said, "Maura, you don't call Daddy by his first name." Maura responded with, "But, why? That's what everyone else calls him." "Maura," my wife said, "you are the only girl in the whole world that gets to call him Daddy."

There are an infinite number of reasons to worship God. We have so many things to be thankful for. He blesses us abundantly. Being a child of God is not something to be taken lightly. A relationship with God has enormous significance. He has given us the privilege and honor of calling Him Father. The fact that we have a loving Creator who died in our place, who adopted us into His family, and who will never turn His back on us, should be all the reason we need to dedicate every aspect of our lives to His glory. We must never forget this.

TAKE ACTION

Take a moment and make a list of all the ways God has been there for you. How has God blessed you? Think back to your childhood, your relationships, and your salvation. Making a list like this helps us remember all that God has done in our lives and shows that He is worth our worship.

IN REVIEW

1. God is the master of restoration.

2. The Devil knows that he cannot stop us from worshipping, and he has no intention to. He loves when we worship, as long as it is not Jesus.

3. We serve a God who desires to be worshipped, but He must be worshipped correctly.

4. An action without affection for God means nothing.

5. God is not interested in part-time Christians. He does not even want you to clock out.

6. You cannot worship God with the same mouth you curse your brother or sister with.

7. God sees our entire life as an act of worship.

8. Sin will eventually leave you empty 100 percent of the time.

9. The emptiness of sin can be a road sign that points you to God.

10. We get the honor and privilege of calling God "father."

Body Language

reDefined: Love

"Believers are never told to become one; we already are one and are expected to act like it."

Joni Eareckson Tada

But speaking the truth in love, let us grow in every way into him who is the head—Christ. From him the whole body, fitted and knit together by every supporting ligament, promotes the growth of the body for building up itself in love by the proper working of each individual part. **(Ephesians 4:15–16), CSB**.

MORE THAN A FEELING

The word "love" can be a difficult word to define. It is a universal desire for every human. When defining love romantically, you can search the web and find volumes of books on the subject. There is an endless number of music albums dedicated to romance. We all want someone in our lives who will be there for us no matter what happens.

Regarding parental love, experts give advice on how to raise your children lovingly. When it comes to desire, chefs publish cookbooks with instructions on how to make your most beloved meals.

This is one of the negative aspects of the English language. We recycle words. This is the case with "love." The multiple meanings, and lack of differentiation between these meanings, allow us to both diminish and exaggerate the word. We reuse love for anything we have affection for.

I *love* my wife.

I *love* my children.

I *love* my dog.

I *love* lasagna.

Obviously, loving my wife and loving lasagna should be expressed in different ways. If the love I have for my wife is the same as the love for my favorite food, how I feel about my wife is really not that great. The love for a spouse comes with obligations that do not exist for something edible. How does the Bible distinguish between these definitions?

The core tenant of the Christian faith is love. First and foremost, we are to love God in every aspect of our lives. Matthew 22:37–38 shows us how foundational our love for God is: *"He said to him, 'Love the Lord your God with all your heart, with all your soul, and with all your mind. This is the greatest and most important command.'"*

Secondly, loving God means loving the people He created. Matthew 22:39–40 concludes its instruction on love by saying, *"The second is like it: Love your neighbor as yourself. All the Law and the Prophets depend on these two commands."* This is the entire objective of Christianity, to love God and love others.

If I had to simplify a biblical definition of love, I would define it as, "Putting someone else before yourself." The life of Jesus was the epitome of how love should look in action. In Him, we see someone who lived a life dedicated to putting others before Himself. He spoke the message of truth, He healed, He served, and He willingly gave up His life in our place. He took the penalty that we deserve.

We are to model the life of Jesus Christ in how we treat others. Our entire faith is built upon this concept. It should be what separates us from the rest of the world. In fact, it was love that served as the best evangelical tool for the early church in the book of Acts. Nancy Pearcey says:

> In the days of the early church, the thing that most impressed their neighbors in the Roman Empire was the community of love they witnessed among believers. "Behold how they love one another," it was said. In every age, the most persuasive evidence of the gospel is not words or arguments but a living demonstration of God's character through Christians' love for one another, expressed in both their words and their actions.[20]

If love is what sets us apart, why is the American Church losing its influence in the culture around us? Why are we seen as unloving and cold to those outside the four walls of the Church? I believe there are two reasons: 1) The world has become better at showing love, or, at least, it is perceived to be. 2) We have given the opportunity away.

The first point is evident when watching the show Shark Tank. This is one of my favorite shows. I enjoy seeing the innovation of products followed by negotiation. One day, I picked up on something I had never noticed before, especially in the younger generation of inventors and entrepreneurs that presented their ideas on the show. A majority of them would donate a portion of their revenue to some kind of charity or non-profit organization. Buying their product meant

---

20 Pearcey, Nancy. *Total Truth*, p. 378.

supporting things like inner-city youth, environmental preservation, wounded military soldiers, etc. These companies made loving acts part of their business model.

I would never say that this is a bad thing. Christian or not, helping others is great and should be commended. My point is that this used to be what the Church was known for. Now people and organizations are doing the things that used to be synonymous with Christianity. There is one key difference though. The difference is that they are doing the loving acts without the accompaniment of the message. Believers use acts of love as the catalyst by which we share the Gospel of Jesus. Sadly, I believe we are falling short of doing both.

The second reason we are losing our influence in the culture around us deals with giving the opportunity away. If it is a privilege to love others through acts of kindness with the hope of showing them Christ, why do we willingly give it up? Why are we allowing others to do the things we are called to do?

I see this a lot in how people now view the government. It used to be that the Church was the entity that helped the poor and the helpless. The widows and the orphans (James 1:27). The ones who had nothing.

Now, the government has taken over that role and we allow it. If someone requires assistance, they turn to the government, not the Church. This is tragic. The government has become a god to so many non-believers and believers alike. We must take back our obligation and cease viewing it as a burden that someone, or something else, needs to bear. God allows us to serve others. We get the joy of putting people before ourselves. We get the honor of showing love.

In neglecting our duties as the Church, our society has mutated and deformed the meaning of love. Love and tolerance are now defined as the same thing. Tolerance has become the standard by which others should be treated.

Even tolerance has shifted in meaning. Christians are supposed to tolerate those outside the faith. We are still supposed to love those who hold different views. We are never called to force our faith on others. But society no longer allows a difference of opinion. Certain views are considered superior. Being tolerant now means the validation of actions that you disagree with. Our culture of tolerance has started punishing biblical beliefs, labeling them as intolerant and hateful.

This mindset prevents love from happening. Scripture never shows love to be silent. It speaks up when someone needs to hear something. Love pushes us to action when we see someone doing something detrimental to their well-being. Believers are to see lost souls destined for hell as those in need of love. They need to be told, even at the cost of being labeled intolerant. They need to know that sin is their master, and it is preventing them from spiritual life.

While tolerance has become destructive to the interaction of Christians and non-Christians, we must realize that this is also taking place within the Church. Many Churches have a high tolerance for sin. Many believers never say to a fellow brother or sister in Christ what they need to hear. They allow them to live in sin and grow further away from Christ.

In the next two chapters, we will be discussing how the Church has redefined the word love. Chapter 7 will deal with what it looks like to show love to those who are outside of the Church by way of Evangelism. I think it is important, though, to first talk about what love looks like within the Church to fellow believers. If we have any hope of showing love to the world, we have to begin by loving each other. Love is the language the Body of Christ should be speaking.

THE SOURCE

Loving correctly begins by going to the source, the origin of love. The Bible proclaims that God is love (1 John 4:16). It is not simply a characteristic. It is not something that He has to try and do. Who He is and how He expresses Himself is love. It is His entire identity.

The primary reason I believe the Church is lacking in love is that we do not go to God. Falling more in love with God results in loving others more. We will not grow in our love for others if we do not pray. If we do not consistently read the Scripture. If we do not approach the Lord regularly. It seems basic, but seeking God is the fundamental first step in living a life of love.

A couple of years ago, a group of my friends and I decided to watch a UFC (Ultimate Fighting Championship) Pay-Per-View. We all chipped in to cover the cost. My friend, who hosted the event at his house, borrowed a 50-inch flat-screen television from the church. We were all set to have a great night of food and entertainment.

On the night of the fight, all the guys showed up only to be disappointed by one little oversight; my friend had forgotten the power cord to the TV. It had completely slipped his mind. We were all disappointed. Everything seemed right. We had the TV, the snacks, and good company. All of that meant nothing though because we did not have one little cord. One small mistake ruined the entire night.

It may seem minor and insignificant, but the cord was everything. This is the case with our spiritual lives. Seeking God is the "cord" that we need in order to have effective lives for ministry. We seek Him through prayer and hearing from His word. It is impossible to grow without these things. Listen to what John Piper says about prayer, "Prayer is the breathing of Christianity. If you don't care about breathing, you don't care about life. If you don't care about prayer, you don't care about spiritual life."

Tapping into the source of love is the way we increase in love. It is the way our hearts change to be more like Christ. 1 John 4:9–11 says:

God's love was revealed among us in this way: God sent his one and only Son into the world so that we might live through him. Love consists in this: not that we loved God, but that he loved us and sent his son to be the atoning sacrifice for our sins. Dear friends, if God loved us in this way, we also must love one another.

I heard a story recently that I felt was a perfect illustration of God's love. An organization called Operation Underground Railroad was founded by a man named Tim Ballard. His goal in starting the operation was to bring awareness and help rescue children out of the sex trafficking industry.

He tells of a time when he was asked to help find and rescue a little boy from Haiti who had been abducted from his church in which his father was the pastor. The country of Haiti is number three in the world, per capita, when it comes to child sex trafficking. Ballard assured the boy's family that he would do everything in his power and never stop trying to find their child. They eventually received word that he was being held, along with other children, in a building that was believed to be an orphanage. There were twenty-eight children total.

After doing surveillance, they felt confident that the little boy was there. Ballard and his team went in and arrested all the men who had kidnapped and were selling these children. They looked throughout the entire complex only to be met with devastating news; the little boy they were looking for was not there.

Ballard described that at that moment he was overcome with a variety of emotions. He was happy that they had rescued twenty-eight children but sad the little boy was still missing. The father was in a different building waiting for Ballard to come through the door holding his child. How was he going to tell this father that they had not found the boy? They had gotten their hopes up for nothing. When Ballard walked through the door empty-handed, the father fell down crying. Ballard said it was the most difficult and inspiring conversation he had ever had with a human being. Inspiring because of how the father responded next.

As the father was sobbing, Ballard mentioned that they had rescued twenty-eight children. Suddenly, the father looked up and wiped the tears from his eyes. He said, "This is great news. You were able to save that many children?"

Ballard did not know how to respond. "Yeah, but we didn't find your son." What the father said next was powerful.

"Yes, but if my son had not been kidnapped, none of those kids would have had a chance. His kidnapping led to this. If I had to give up my son so that those twenty-eight kids could be rescued, then that is a burden I am willing to bear."

How does someone respond this way? How can someone see past their own turmoil to see the goodness of God? This father was tapping into the true source of love. It is the only way he could have responded in such a godly manner. He was looking past himself and putting others first. Amid such pain and sorrow, he was able to find joy in the rescue of others.

It is worth noting that this father informed the government officials that he was willing to adopt any of the twenty-eight children who could not find homes. In the end, he and his wife adopted eight of them. Ballard and his wife adopted two. Since the time of this story, Operation Underground Railroad has rescued over three thousand victims from slavery.

BODY LANGUAGE

The human body is an amazing creation. How our bodies operate and keep us alive is fascinating. Here are some interesting facts you may not know.

1. The heart circulates blood through the body about one thousand times a day.

2. Pound for pound, your bones are stronger than steel.

3. You are taller in the morning than you are at night.

4. A sneeze blows air out of your nose at one hundred miles per hour.

5. Infants are born with approximately three hundred bones, but as they grow, some of these bones fuse together. By the time they reach adulthood, they only have two hundred and six bones.

The creative genius of God is seen when observing the human body and all that it is capable of. Many passages of Scripture compare the Church to a body (1 Corinthians 12:12). Like the human body, when the Church body is working the way it should, amazing things happen.

After Jesus resurrected and ascended to heaven, believers were filled with the Holy Spirit at Pentecost (Acts 2). Since that time, the Church has become how the Gospel is spread throughout the world. Jesus came with a message when He walked the Earth, and we are to continue that proclamation.

Jesus was the human body in which God dwelled. The Church is the body by which the Spirit of God dwells. The Church body is to speak a language and that language is love. While believers make up the different parts of the body, Jesus is the head.

Francis Schaeffer pointed out the importance of recognizing what Christ is when compared to a body.

> The human body is directed by the head. The hands are not in direct relationship with each other. The reason they cooperate is that each of the hands, each of the joints, each of the fingers, is under the control of a single control point, and that is the head. Block the body from the head and

the body is spastic; the fingers, for example, could never find each other, and uniformity of action would come to an end.[21]

Christ, being the head, is what dictates the movement and action of the Church. This is important to recognize and remember. How we interact with one another should be determined by the direction of God. It is not uncommon in the American Church to see "hands" fighting with other "hands." "Legs" getting upset with "ankles." The point being, a body can only be unified if it is being directed by the head.

This is the mindset we need to return to. Sadly, I believe many Christians are not taking direction from the head. We are being led by other things. This is a great question to ask yourself. What is leading you? What determines what love looks like to you? What determines your direction?

This brings us to how the language of love is being spoken within the Church body. When allowing the head to direct the body, the love of Christ should permeate every aspect of the Church. When we are led by something else, love is absent. This is what we are seeing today. Loveless churches.

In the chapter on sin (chapter 4), we discussed the importance of having a high view of what offends God. This high view allows us to see sin for what it really is. To adjust our lifestyles by following the Bible. Sin is running rampant within the American Church because we do not love each other enough to call it out. It is not something that only exists outside the Church. It is thriving and growing within. We tolerate and avoid it. It is easy to overlook someone's sin. It is difficult to point out when someone has missed the mark because it is awkward. It can change or end a friendship. But this is precisely why we have such a sin problem in our churches today.

---

21 Schaeffer, Francis. *True Spirituality*, p. 146.

Sin within the Church is nothing new. Paul had to deal with it in the churches he planted. The Corinthian church had believers doing all kinds of sinful acts. The believers in Corinth were from a culture that was saturated with immorality. In fact, sexual sin was so rampant that when a woman from another nation was promiscuous, people would refer to her as a "Corinthian woman." Corinth had an image, and it was not a godly one. Unfortunately, this sin crept into the Church and needed to be addressed by Paul. The phrase "everything is permissible to me" (1 Corinthians 6:12) was commonly used by Corinthian believers as a way of taking advantage of God's grace. The mindset was that by God's grace they were forgiven of all sins. Past, present, and future. They felt this forgiveness gave them free rein to literally do whatever they wanted resulting in the spread of sin within the Church. Sexual sin was so prevalent that Paul said it "wasn't even tolerated among pagans" (1 Corinthians 5:5).

This was unacceptable to Paul, and it should be unacceptable for us today. The sins that we deal with inside the American Church are not very different. Divorce, pornography, gossip, slander, anger, resentment, selfishness, etc. We should not tolerate this invasion of sin within the Church. It is a cancer that is eating away at the body, and often we do nothing about it. Instead, we misuse verses like Luke 6:37 that tell us not to judge.

Pointing out someone's sin is not judgment. It is the most loving thing you can do for a believer. Robert Cheong and Robert Jones said that "when we are entangled with sin, regardless of the reason, we tend to question God's love for us while being blinded to His glorious presence, promises, and power."[22] Why would we possibly want someone to continue living this way?

When it comes to non-Christians, we are to point out general sin. With believers, we are to point out specific sin. Why? To bring them back to fellowship with God. To help them remove the obstacle of sin

---

22 Kellemen, Bob. *Biblical Counseling and the Church*, p. 157.

that would prevent them from living the abundant life. Our fear of confrontation is preventing closeness to God. It is creating division. It is giving the Church an image that looks very similar to the world around us.

FAMILY MATTERS

So, what can be done? How can we fix the sin problem within the Church? I believe the answer is love. Is this not what Jesus taught? John 13:13 says, *"I give you a new command: Love one another. Just as I have loved you, you are also to love one another."*

A biblical view of love is necessary. We must stop letting the world redefine what love truly is. Godly love is obligatory. It often involves difficult conversations; it does not avoid them. In love, we address the problem. In love, we confront a believer who is sinning and point them back to God. In love, we show sinning believers what the Bible says, even when it is hard to hear. This process is called Church discipline and it is something rarely practiced anymore.

The passage in which we are instructed about Church discipline is Matthew 18:15–17. It says:

> *If your brother sins against you, go tell him his fault, between you and him alone. If he listens to you, you have won your brother. But if he won't listen, take one or two others with you, so that by the testimony of two or three witnesses every fact may be established. If he doesn't pay attention to them, tell the Church. If he doesn't pay attention even to the Church, let him be like a Gentile and a tax collector to you.*

It is important to first realize that these verses are dealing with family. People within the body of Christ. In his book *Letters to the Church*, Francis Chan points out the priority of the Church family:

> Pushing the Church to live as a family is not some gimmick, some flavor of "church" that would be fun to try; it's commanded. And it's offered. Crafting the Church into a truly united and supernaturally loving family is the very thing God is wanting to do.[23]

God desires this of us because no one loves like family. I am always amazed when I see a hardened criminal sitting in front of a judge waiting to hear the verdict. No matter what he has done, no matter the enormity of his crime, his mother is always there to support him. She does not support the fact that he has broken the law; she supports him. In her eyes, he is still her son, her baby. This is the bond of family and the bond that God desires for all believers who are a part of His family.

Being adopted into God's family means we have brothers and sisters we did not have before. Think of the benefit of that. Paul David Tripp says:

> So often, the blessing of adoption is seen only through an individualistic lens: I am a child of God. This is true, but your adoption goes beyond an individual blessing. You have been adopted into a new family.[24]

We have a blessing and responsibility to our brothers and sisters in Christ. This view of family should move us to action. When an offense happens, it is up to the spiritual family to deal with it. When we approach someone guilty of sin, we are not going to condemn. We are going to help them refocus on God. We are going in hopes of helping repair their Christian walk. We do this with Scripture. We show them what the source of love has to say on the matter.

The second step, in Matthew 18, occurs when the person in sin does not accept what is being said. They do not see their wrong and

---

23 Chan, Francis. *Letters to the Church*, p. 80.
24 Lane, Timothy and Tripp, Paul David. *How People Change*, p. 70.

continue to live in opposition to God. We are then instructed to take two or three people and confront them a second time. Why is this? What is the point of bringing other people into the situation? This is done to validate what the Bible says about their sin.

In love, we are to use Scripture to point out sin. We confront because the sin is against God. His Word shows us the offense. If we point out the sin with Scripture and are still ignored, or accused of seeing the Scripture incorrectly, we are to then bring in others to determine who is accurately interpreting what the Bible says. If the person still disagrees, even after multiple people verify what the Word of God says on the matter, we are to go before the Church. These steps are taken in hopes of bringing the person back into fellowship with the Lord. In hopes of helping them correctly see what God says.

It is important to realize that when a person is removed from the Church, it is not because they broke a rule. It is not that they did something that God cannot forgive. It is because they refused to see what God says. They refused to give up a sin that is keeping them from fellowship with the Lord. A person who is actively living in sin, even after being shown the truth, is not someone who should represent Christ with a church membership.

I can honestly say that I hate going through the process of Church discipline, however, I often love the results. I have had awkward and difficult conversations that have resulted in closer friendships. They have resulted in someone coming to love the Lord more than they did before. I have been confronted by a believer over a sin I harbored. I now look back with appreciation that a brother in Christ cared for me enough to speak the truth.

The image of the Body of Christ is at stake. The spirituality of fellow believers is on the line. We must stop tolerating sin in the Church. Keeping each other accountable is the most loving thing we can do for one another. Keeping each other accountable is the most beneficial thing we can do for the image of Christianity.

TAKE ACTION

Do an honest assessment of your pursuit of God. Write down some ways in which you can seek Him more. Do you have a daily quiet time that involves prayer and Scripture reading? Do you set aside time to worship Him? I have heard it said before that what you value most, you will schedule. We must seek out the source of love, but sadly, many Christians do not schedule a daily interaction with Him. They do it if they can "find the time." Reserve a time of day specifically for God.

Is there a brother or sister in Christ that you need to confront? Is there someone in your life who professes Christ as their Savior, yet harbors a sin that is damaging their spiritual walk with the Lord? If so, pray that God will give you the boldness to confront them in love.

IN REVIEW

1. The core tenant of the Christian faith is love.

2. The life of Jesus was the epitome of how love should look in action.

3. We get the joy of putting people before ourselves. We get the honor of showing love.

4. While tolerance has become destructive to the interaction between Christians and non-Christians, we must realize that this is also taking place within the Church.

5. Falling more in love with God results in loving others more.

6. Like the human body, when the Church body is working the way it should, amazing things happen.

7. Jesus was the human body in which God dwelled. The Church is the body by which the Spirit of God dwells.

8. When it comes to non-Christians, we are to point out general sin. With believers, we are to point out specific sin.

9. We have a blessing and responsibility to our brothers and sisters in Christ.

10. Keeping each other accountable is the most beneficial thing we can do for the image of Christianity.

7:

Why Are You Silent?

reDefined: Evangelism

"You are not only responsible for what you say, but also for what you do not say."

Martin Luther

When he saw the crowds, he felt compassion for them, because they were distressed and dejected, like sheep without a shepherd. Then he said to his disciples, "The harvest is abundant, but the workers are few. Therefore, pray to the Lord of the harvest to send out workers into his harvest. (**Matthew 9:36–38**), **CSB**.

THE GREATEST MOMENT

What is the best thing that has ever happened to you? Typically, this moment is something not kept private. It is something you want to share with everyone around you. Once you find the love of your life, you shout it from the rooftops. The birth of your child is something you post all over your social media. When your favorite college football team wins the national championship, you let the world know. These great moments are impossible to keep to ourselves.

When it comes to being a Christian, it should be no different. Think of the day you gave your life to Christ. Think of the joy you experienced knowing that Jesus saved you from spiritual death. I love seeing the excitement of new believers who share their conversion with anyone who will listen. They love the Lord and do not care who knows it. It is the greatest moment of their life and nothing else comes close.

If this is the case with every Christian, why are so many of them silent about it? If we have the greatest message known to man, why do we keep it to ourselves? Kirk Cameron once said, "If you had the cure to cancer, wouldn't you share it? You have the cure to death … get out there and share it." Unfortunately, this is not happening.

According to bible.org, 95 percent of all American Christians have never led anyone to Christ. Eighty-one percent do not consistently witness about Jesus. Less than 2 percent are involved in the ministry of evangelism. Ninety-three percent of all church growth is transfer growth. Let me say that again. Ninety-three percent of new people attending church are not people who are new to the faith. They are Christians who left their old church to find a new one. Often, they were fed up with the way their last church was operating and found a different church that fit their preferences.

These statistics are staggering. The Bible tells us to be loud with our faith. To share it. Yet, we are silent. Why is this? Could it be that the American Church lacks the same motivation as Jesus?

YOUR MOTIVATION

Everyone is motivated by something. I love watching the Olympics and seeing American athletes compete for our country. There is just something about watching someone give their all when they go up against the rest of the world. This is why so many people love the Rocky movies. He is the underdog who is motivated to make a name for himself. That motivation is what fueled him to go through all the work and training of preparing for the next fight. If he was not motivated, he never would have beaten Ivan Drago in Rocky IV (the best of all the Rocky movies).

People are motivated by different things. Some have made family the most important thing in life. Others have chosen their careers. Have you ever sat down and asked yourself: What motivates me? What is your main drive in life? If you could do anything, what would you do with your time?

These are great questions to ask yourself because the answers show what you consider to be most important. It tells you what you value above all. Things like family, career, and politics are not bad in themselves. These are great things to invest in. But as Christians, should these things be the main motivation for our lives? Those are things people outside of the Church are also passionate about. Should believers and non-believers share the same motivation in life?

The sad truth is that a lot of Christians are motivated by things that do not matter to God. As someone who follows Christ, you should strive to have the same passion in life as Jesus. So, what was His passion? What was it that made Jesus come to Earth, serve, heal, and finally die on a cross in our place?

The answer is people.

Jesus left heaven for the lost. While He was on the cross, you were on His mind. That is what motivated Jesus. He was passionate about proclaiming the truth to those who needed to hear it. God is most glorified when people turn from their sinful ways and give themselves to Him.

This chapter is about accurately defining evangelism. Sadly, many churches in America do not have a biblical view of what it means to share the Gospel. Evangelism has been reduced. It has become watered down. I am convinced that if Jesus was walking the earth today, He would live out His faith differently than most of us. What a terrible thought. If the Bible compels us to act like Christ, why do so many Christians look nothing like Him?

Jesus left heaven to bring us a message, but many Christians will never take that message outside the four walls of the Church. Evangelism has been inverted. We no longer reach out, we bring in. The news that non-believers so desperately need to hear has become reserved for those who walk through the doors of the Church. It is only proclaimed on Sunday mornings. This is not how it is supposed to be. We completely miss the point when we see our Sunday services as the primary tool of evangelism.

Redefining evangelism this way has birthed negative results. First, it takes the privilege of sharing the Gospel away from those not in full-time ministry. Someone once told me that he invited a friend to church because he wanted his friend to hear the Gospel. His statement led me to ask, "Why haven't you told him?" Hear me, I love seeing non-believers in Church. It is an opportunity to witness the Body of Christ in fellowship and worship. But this should not be the only place someone hears about God. Do not let your pastor be the only one who gets the honor of sharing the Good News. God has put you in a specific place at a specific time with specific people around you that need to hear the Gospel. Do not miss the opportunity.

Another negative result of seeing evangelism as something that happens only on Sundays is that it waters down our church services. Realize that the gathering of Christians was established for the edification and fellowship of believers (Acts 2:42). In the book of Acts, evangelism happened outside of these gatherings. Think about what this does to our services when we see them only as evangelistic. Our mindset becomes, "What can we do that will draw non-believers into our building?" This way of thinking typically results in shallow teaching and performance-based worship.

Pastors should be teaching the body of believers how to take the message out into the world. Worship is for Christians, not unbelievers. Who cares if the style of music reaches those who have never given their lives to Christ (This is coming from someone who loves loud, upbeat worship music)? Worship is not about preference; it is about reverence. Non-believers cannot give anything to God if they have not first given their lives. So why do we focus our worship services on non-believers if they are unable to worship?

Evangelism should and must happen outside of our corporate gatherings on Sundays. Our lifestyles should proclaim what we know about Jesus. This only happens when we share the same motivation as Christ. We have to love people the way Jesus did. Do you have this same motivation?

GET ANGRY

The word "compassion" is used many times in Scripture when describing how Jesus felt toward the people He was ministering to. After seeing those who were sick, both physically and spiritually, He had a strong desire to rescue them. This word is typically used today to describe a person who has sympathy, pity, or concern for those who are less fortunate. Mother Teresa was known as compassionate for how she treated the poor. Several missionaries could also be described this way for how they dedicated their lives to the lost.

I am reminded of another place in Scripture where Jesus is described as compassionate. He was having a conversation with a leper who desired to be healed. Mark 1:41 says, *"Moved with compassion, Jesus reached out His hand and touched him. 'I am willing,' he told him. 'Be made clean.'"*

Most translations use the phrase, "moved with compassion", or something similar, to describe Jesus' attitude at the moment. Other translations, instead, use the phrase, "becoming angry." Anger and compassion are not two words that are generally associated together as they appear to contradict. So, which one is correct? Was Jesus angry or compassionate? It depends on which Greek manuscript you are referencing. There is debate as to which translation is the correct one.

If I am being honest, that debate does not interest me. I believe both translations are accurate to the character of Christ. We obviously see the compassion of Jesus in multiple passages (Matthew 15:32; Mark 6:34; Luke 19:41–42). But what about anger? What would enrage Jesus when seeing the leper? This can be illustrated with a story about two of my children.

My son Jack is my second-born. He is a creative kid who likes to build things. My son Peter, the third-born, likes to break things. We often call him the "wrecking ball." One day, my wife called for my boys to eat dinner but only Jack came down. She asked where Peter was, and before Jack could respond, we heard the noise of Lego pieces crashing down the stairs. We soon realized that the pieces belonged to a car that Jack had built earlier in the day.

He stood motionless. After a moment of silence, Jack walked over to the stairs to find Peter standing at the top. He was the one who threw it. Jack was devastated. He had literally put hours into building this car and all his hard work now lay in pieces at his feet. The tears did not last long though. His face went from sad to angry in seconds. My wife had to jump up and prevent Jack from destroying his little brother.

What was it that caused Jack to be angry? The answer is simple. His creation, the thing he spent so much time and energy building, was broken. After it was thrown down the stairs, it became flawed and looked nothing like it originally did. In his opinion, Jack had created the perfect car and this provoked him to anger when Peter deformed it.

Jesus was in the same situation. He was a part of creation (John 1:1–3; Hebrews 1:2) at the beginning of time. God defined what perfection is in the Garden of Eden. Even after all the amazing things He created, God finished off with His masterpiece, humanity. The only created thing that bore His image. We were created perfectly. However, this perfection came to an end when Adam and Eve disobeyed God. Sin entered the world and deformed God's perfect creation.

When Jesus looked at this leper, He saw what His masterpiece once was and what sin had done to it. Humanity was never supposed to look like that. Leprosy was not in the garden of Eden. Sickness and death were unknown to Adam and Eve. It was the place of literal perfection. Jesus was provoked to anger over the consequence of sin on mankind. He was enraged at the condition of His creation. This was the reason He came to Earth; He came to restore us.

I believe the Church needs to see sin this way. We need to have compassion for those whom sin has corrupted. We need to be motivated to love people who are under the stronghold of sin. I wish we were more enraged over the Devil's hold on our communities. Over the sin that ravages our country. Over the number of people that will spend eternity separated from God in hell. We must be moved to action. We need to get angry.

ARE YOU QUALIFIED?

The main reason people do not share the Gospel is fear of not knowing the answer. They feel limited in their knowledge and are afraid that they will be asked a question they will not be able to respond to (Unfortunately, a lot of parents fall victim to this fear with their children). Here is a truth for every Christian:

If you have given your life to Christ, you are qualified to share the Gospel.

That is it. Your salvation is the only condition that needs to be met to evangelize. You do not need a Bible degree to tell others about what

Jesus has done for you. You have a story. Tell that story. If you do not feel prepared to share the Gospel, ask yourself if you have ever felt ready or qualified for any of the big things in your life.

The day of my wedding, I felt I was in over my head. That did not stop me from marrying my wife. I remember the day my daughter was born. She was our first child, and we had no idea what to do. That reality fully sank in when the nurse walked us to the front doors of the hospital and then said goodbye. I could not believe it. We had no idea what to do with a child, and they were just going to let us leave the hospital with one. But guess what, we still did it. As unprepared as we felt, we took it head-on. I never knew that being a parent meant I was going to have to learn to be a lifeguard. I have had to save my son Peter from drowning three times, something I never expected and did not prepare for.

Christians need to have this mindset. It does not matter if we do not feel ready. People around us are dying spiritually and we have the answer. We have the message they need to hear but do not tell it because we are too scared. Feeling unqualified has made us silent. Think of all the people with limitations that God used to do amazing things. Moses had a speech impediment. David faced a giant in battle. Gideon led a limited army against a massive enemy. Look at what God was able to do with the early church.

In Acts 8, we read about the severe persecution that had broken out against Christians. This persecution caused the believers to be scattered. One would think that this kind of opposition would hinder the spread of the Gospel. Talk about limitations. Look what happened instead:

> *On that day a severe persecution broke out against the church in Jerusalem, and all except the apostles were scattered throughout the land of Judea and Samaria. Devout men buried Stephen and mourned deeply over him. Saul, however, was ravaging the church. He would enter house after house, drag off men and women, and*

put them in prison. So those who were scattered went on their way preaching the word. (**Acts 8:1–4**), **CSB**.

Do not miss what happened in this passage. When this persecution began, all the believers, except the Apostles, were scattered throughout Judea and Samaria. Those that were scattered were the ones sharing the Gospel and leading people to Christ. The significance lies in the fact that the Apostles stayed in Jerusalem. They were the preachers. The ones who were called to build the foundation of the Church. The ones who personally saw the resurrected Christ and were called by the Holy Spirit to spread the Gospel using signs and wonders. Yet, the Gospel was not being spread throughout Judea and Samaria by them. It was being spread by *"the ones who were scattered."*

We do not know who these people were. We only know that they loved Jesus and spread that news. We do not know their names. We do not know their backgrounds. They were ordinary people with an extraordinary message who did not care about their lack of qualifications. They just did what needed to be done. J.D. Greer said, "The only thing more amazing than how fast the Gospel spread was how anonymous it was."

Can you imagine what Christianity would look like in America today if we had this same kind of motivation? If we did not care who got the credit? If we did not depend on preachers to be the only ones sharing the Gospel? If we did not let fear of being unqualified hold us back? If anyone had the right to fear, it was the early church members who lived every day with the knowledge that they could die for simply loving Jesus.

NO ONE IS OUTSIDE THE LOVE OF GOD

What does it mean to have the same motivation as Jesus? It means that we see people the way He did. He never saw anyone as an outcast or an outsider. Just think about the people He associated with: lepers, adulterers, and tax collectors. Society turned its back on these people and often hated them. Jesus did not. No matter what they did, Jesus responded with love and compassion.

There was a story out of Dallas, Texas, in which a police officer named Amber Guyger shot and killed a man whom she believed to be an intruder in her apartment. She had just gotten off of a fourteen-hour shift and was going home for the night. As she was about to enter her front door, she noticed it was already unlocked and slightly cracked open. Fearing who was inside her home, she pulled out her gun, walked in, and opened fire on the man inside. He was instantly killed.

What makes this story tragic is that breaking and entering never happened. The man inside was not there to rob or harm Amber Guyger. He was there because he lived there. Guyger had mistaken his apartment for her own. The man's name was Botham Jean, and he was shot dead while eating ice cream and watching television in his own home.

The public outcry for justice was understandably loud. Suspicion began to circulate that this was a racist act. Guyger was white and Botham Jean was black. Guyger's defense was that it was a mistake. She was tired and unaware of where she was. It had nothing to do with race.

Even if that was the case, how could she make such a mistake? Botham Jean lived on the floor above her and had a bright red welcome mat outside his apartment. Clearly not Guyger's home. It should have been obvious she was in the wrong place.

Whether it was racism or simply a mistake, justice needed to be served. As the headlines of this story circulated throughout the country, Guyger was seen as an outcast. Someone not worth loving because of the horrible thing she had done. During the trial, something truly amazing happened when Botham Jean's brother, Brandt, took the witness stand.

Sitting before the lady who killed his brother, Brandt forgave her. "Speaking for myself, I love you like anyone else," he said. "I'm not going to say I want you to rot and die. I don't even want you to go to jail. I want the best for you and the best is for you to give your life to Christ. It's what Botham would want you to do. I want you to know that I love you."

Brandt concluded his remarks by turning to the judge and asking if he could give Guyger a hug. As the judge agreed, Brandt left the stand and embraced Amber Guyger who ran toward him drawn to the love and compassion she was given. The only noise in the courtroom was the sound of crying.

What could make a person respond with such compassion? What could cause a man to look at the person who took the life of his brother and say, "I love you"? This only happens when we see others the way Jesus did. Brandt did not see Guyger as unlovable or outside the love of God. What we have done in the past does not matter to Jesus. Praise God that He will overlook every terrible thing we have done and still stand there with open arms.

It is almost impossible to watch that video and not tear up like the people in the courtroom. I imagine Guyger felt all alone in the world. I imagine she felt as if everyone hated her. When we have the same motivation as Christ, the unlovable outcasts of this world will come to know that there is a God who loves them no matter what. We cannot let our anger prevent us from acting the way Brandt did.

WHY ARE YOU SILENT?

I am the true vine, and my Father is the gardener. Every branch in me that does not produce fruit he removes, and he prunes every branch that produces fruit so that it will produce more fruit. You are already clean because of the word I have spoken to you. Remain in me, and I in you. Just as a branch is unable to produce fruit by itself unless it remains on the vine, neither can you unless you remain in me. I am the vine; you are the branches. The one who remains in me and I in him produces much fruit, because you can do nothing without me. **(John 15:1–5), CSB.**

You do not have a relationship with God. This passage shows us the vitality of fellowship with God. If you are living a life of silence regarding the Gospel, the first step is to diagnose your relationship with the Lord. Are you connected to God as the branch is to the vine? Does your Christian walk produce any kind of spiritual fruit? If the answer is no, you have a relationship problem.

I have heard many preachers talk about the importance of exhibiting the fruits of the Spirit talked about in Ephesians 5:22–23. There are multitudes of sermons on how to be more patient, kind, and joyful. This way of thinking though can be problematic. The fruits of the Spirit are merely evidence. Proof of our relationship with God. However, they are not the things we are to strive for. When we grow in our relationship with God, the fruit will come naturally.

Is your love for God growing? Like any relationship, growth is determined by fellowship. It is determined by spending time together. A young couple in love wants to experience every moment together in hopes of fully knowing each other. It takes communication. This is why we have Scripture. The Bible is a gift from God so that we can know Him.

The problem is that so many Christians silence the voice of God in their lives by refusing to open their Bibles. They merely collect dust on the shelf. How do we expect to share the love of God with others when we are not growing in our love for God? We must seek Him daily. We must desire to grow closer to Him. Only then will we have the passion to spread the Gospel.

You are not passionate about what God is passionate about. In the movie *Catch Me If You Can*, the main character is a con artist named Frank. He would act as a professional in multiple fields, convincing others that he was who he said he was. After stealing a lot of money, he ended up getting arrested by the FBI. While in prison, an agent got the brilliant idea that Frank could be of some help to the bureau.

Frank was tested to observe his knowledge. He was given a counterfeit check to see if he could notice it was a fake. After holding the check for mere seconds, he instantly knew it was a counterfeit. During his criminal life, he had become an expert on what real checks looked like. He needed to know the real to create the fake.

When reading through the Bible, we see what Christianity really is. We do not have to guess; it is spelled out for us. Do we look anything like the early Church in the book of Acts? People believe that Christianity is all about going to church, giving 10 percent of your income, and serving in a ministry. As long as you are doing one, or all of these things, you are a good Christian.

Do not get me wrong, these things are great. However, the mission of Christianity, what matters most to the believer, should be spreading the Gospel to those who do not know Jesus. Like Christ, the early Church was most passionate about lost souls. This is how we tell the real from the fake. Are you concerned more about your growth or someone else giving their life to Jesus? These things are not supposed to be separate. The spiritual growth of a believer should result in the proclamation of the Gospel. Billy Graham once said, "Our faith becomes stronger as we express it; a growing faith is a sharing faith."

THE CRIPPLED BODY

Romans 1:16 says, *"For I am not ashamed of the gospel, because it is the power of God for salvation to everyone who believes, first to the Jew, and also to the Greek."*

I believe many of us underestimate the power of the Gospel. I believe we do not truly think it is capable of making the changes needed in our country. This mindset is crippling us as a church. It is holding us back from living out true Christianity.

The word "power" from the passage above is translated from the Greek word "*dunamis.*" This is where we get the word dynamite. It is an appropriate origin when you think of the power behind a stick of dynamite. Have you ever seen what it does? Dynamite is not something that goes off unnoticed. When it explodes, everyone is aware. Paul is telling us that the Gospel has enormous power.

The Church is called to take the Gospel and, like dynamite, set it off. The reality is most Christians are not lighting the fuse. We cannot expect the lost in our nation to turn to God if they do not witness the explosive power of the Gospel. Unfortunately, many of us have swapped out dynamite for other messages that have the power of a single match. They make a spark or small flame but eventually fizzle out.

This is the case with a message I call "political evangelism." It is a message that has no power yet so many Christians have subscribed. It is the mindset that the most important thing for the American Christian is religious freedom. Our forefathers fought and died for the right to have religious liberties and our current government is taking them away. All of our energy and attention should be dedicated to fighting against this abduction.

The tragedy is that many American believers will go to the ends of the Earth to preserve their religious liberties but will never use them. It is so easy to share the Gospel in the United States, but most do not. In China, believers are being put in prison or losing their lives for sharing the Gospel. They have no religious liberties, but the Gospel is exploding with such power. Chinese Christians are lighting the fuse with little concern over what will happen to them. It is a Church body that is taking the message to those who need it.

The Bible describes the Church as the hands and feet of Jesus. Unfortunately, the American Church body has crippled itself. Are you being the hands and feet that deliver a life-giving message to the spiritually dead? Are you igniting the full power of the Gospel?

YOUR CHAPTER

When my wife and I first got married, we were horribly in debt. We had both taken out student loans to pay for college and the monthly payments had finally kicked in. We had deferred paying them off for some time, but eventually the collectors came calling. Knowing we could not live this way, we joined a class in hopes of learning to manage our finances. It was a nine-week course.

The first two weeks were great. We went to the class and interacted with other couples who were in the same situation. We did all the homework and were finally starting to feel hopeful that our life of debt was going to be short-lived. Due to sickness, we had to miss the third session but came back for the fourth. We never missed another week.

After completing the course, we were ready. We had hope. It was time to get out of debt. However, we made no progress. We tried everything we learned but still could not get ahead. About four months later we ran into a couple who had gone through the class. They were doing great. They were paying off debt and saving for retirement. We asked them what the secret was. We asked them how they were finding success. It was simple, they stuck to their budget.

My wife and I could not remember learning about a budget. The couple then informed us that the course taught about budgeting on the third session, the one we missed. The entire course hinged on the information we missed when we were out sick. We immediately called up the instructor and got the notes and video for that third week and it changed our attack on debt. After five long years of sticking to the budget, we paid off our last student loan and became debt-free. Our success would not have happened if it were not for week three.

Whether you know it or not, your life is telling a story. Our lives are small sections within the big picture of God's narrative. If the story of eternity is a multi-volume book, our contribution might amount to a mere chapter or paragraph. The speck of time we occupy pales in comparison to all of history and what is to come. However, even as small as your story may be, it is not insignificant. Your chapter, or paragraph, might be the "budgeting" section that someone needs to hear that will lead them to Christ. You should never look past the importance of where God has placed you. You are where you are because God put you there, even if your contribution to God's story may only be a single word or sentence.

The famous preacher D.L. Moody came to know Christ in the back of a shoe store. While he was working, his Sunday School teacher came in and shared the Gospel with him. After giving his life to Christ, Moody went into ministry. It has been estimated that Moody preached directly to one hundred million people without the means of technology we have today.

Think of all the people who know Moody's name and reputation but have no idea who his Sunday School teacher was. I cannot imagine that his teacher could have predicted the number of salvations that would happen simply as a result of sharing the Gospel with a young man in the back of a shoe store. We have no idea the eternal impact we can have in God's story if we simply mirror what Jesus came to do, share the good news with those who are spiritually dead. Do not miss the opportunities that God has placed before you. Do not waste your chapter.

TAKE ACTION

God has put you where you are for a reason. Write down the names of some people you know who need to hear about Jesus, people that are in your circle of influence (work, school, neighborhood, family, etc.). Pray for them continually. When you are around them, do not be silent about your faith.

IN REVIEW

1. The sad truth is that a lot of Christians are motivated by things that do not matter to God.

2. While Jesus was on the cross, you were on His mind.

3. Evangelism has been inverted. We no longer reach out, we bring in.

4. Our lifestyles should proclaim what we know about Jesus.

5. If you have given your life to Christ, you are qualified to share the Gospel.

6. Jesus never saw anyone as an outcast or outsider.

7. If you are living a life of silence regarding the Gospel, the first step is to diagnose your relationship with the Lord.

8. Unfortunately, many of us have swapped out dynamite for other messages that have the power of a single match.

9. The American Church body has crippled itself.

10. You are where you are because God put you there, even if your contribution to God's story may only be a single word or sentence.

Just Say No

reDefined: The Abundant Life

"He is no fool who gives what he cannot keep to gain what he cannot lose."

Jim Elliot

Set your minds on things above, not on earthly things.
(**Colossians 3:2**), **CSB**.

A NEW WORD

I want to begin this chapter by teaching you a word. It is a word that everyone knows but rarely uses. When used correctly and often, it is a word that can change your life. It can make you more productive, efficient, a better spouse, a better parent, and most importantly, a better Christian. Are you ready to hear it?

The word is NO.

There are benefits to learning how to say no regularly. I once read an article written by a man who was a project manager at a large company. He was asked to give some advice on how to be more productive. The key to having a productive day, he said, is to sit down and write out the top ten things you need to get done. Once you finish writing that list, cross off the bottom seven and fully focus on the top three. By saying no to the bottom seven, your full attention can be placed on the three most important tasks.

Any parent with children knows the importance of this word. I believe there are times the most loving thing you can say to your child is no. Imagine a world in which we allowed children to have whatever they want. Where we said yes to their every request. Do we really want to live in that kind of world?

My son Jack approached me recently and asked if we could watch TV and play video games all day. As tempting as the offer was, I realized some chores needed to be done and he already had screen time the day before. For these reasons, I told him no. I then heard the classic line, "But my friend's parents let him watch TV all day." Without even thinking I responded with, "Well, his parents don't love him." Obviously, I was joking, but we have to realize that giving in and saying yes is not always the best response.

At the beginning of every year, there is a large emphasis placed on saying yes to things. We call them New Year's resolutions. We promise ourselves that we are going to say yes to more exercise, to have a better attitude, to pray, and read our Bibles more. We will say yes to spending more time with our families. These are all great things that need to happen. However, I want this chapter to go in the opposite direction. I want to focus on the things the Bible tells us to say no to.

When reading Scripture, we are told that the Christian is going to live a life of constant struggle. The sinful nature we are born with is in continual opposition to God. The Devil wants us to say yes to the sinful things that come our way, things like anger, lust, and pride. To grow in our relationship with Christ, we have to say no to these things. I believe that the word NO is necessary in order to grow in your relationship with Christ. I believe that the word NO is necessary to have the abundant life the Bible promises to believers.

BOUNDARIES

I have had people tell me that their rejection of Christianity is based on the number of rules. They see it as a religion that hinders a person from living life to the fullest, that God will punish those who step out of line. This is a massive distortion of God's character. The gross misrepresentation of Christianity today is the suggestion that God is only interested in stopping us from being happy, that His job is to tell us no to everything we ask.

The first step to overcoming this mindset is the realization of our sinful natures (Romans 5:12). We are compelled to do things that go against what God wants. Without Jesus, we have no choice but to rebel against Him. This is not something we are taught. We do not have to learn how to sin. It is corruption that is natural to us.

Even though we are born with this nature, we are damaged spiritually when we give in to it. Sin separates us from God. In love, He tells us what sin is, allowing us to choose to follow Him or not.

Our current culture tells us to act upon our sinful desires with no fear of the consequences. This is especially true when it comes to sex. We are told that sex is great when it is done free of connection or relationship. Sleep with as many people as you want. Do not hold yourself back by committing to one person. Do not miss out on the experience.

The result of this misguided thinking has left many people empty and broken. God has given humanity the gift of sex, but when done incorrectly, it has devastating consequences. Out of His love for us,

God has set up boundaries for sex allowing us to experience this gift in its fullness. Study after study shows that people consider themselves more sexually satisfied when it is done within the context of a committed marriage; the way God intended for it to be.

We should not see these boundaries as negative. In the same way that a guardrail prevents you from running your car off the road, God's boundaries, or rules, are established to help us stay the course, to help us live life the way God desires, an abundant life. John 10:10 says, *"The thief comes only to steal and kill and destroy. I came that they may have life and have it abundantly."*

Unfortunately, like the other words we have discussed, the promise of abundant life has taken on a different meaning. I get angry when I hear preachers inaccurately proclaim that abundant life means monetary gain or physical health: "Turn to God and He will bless you with wealth beyond your wildest imagination. Give your life to Jesus and He will heal all your sickness."

We are never promised those things on this side of heaven. They may happen, they may not. Those are eternal rewards waiting for us guaranteed by our salvation.

While we still walk the earth, we must remember that there is an enemy who wants us out of fellowship with God. He will do everything in his power to stop us from growing in our faith. It is for this reason that we should be on guard. We should be aware of the attacks that will come our way and resist them. We must learn to say NO.

SAY NO TO IDOLATRY

If then you have been raised with Christ, seek the things that are above, where Christ is, seated at the right hand of God. Set your minds on things that are above, not on things that are on

earth. For you have died, and your life is hidden with Christ in
God. When Christ who is your life appears, then you also will
appear with him in glory. Put to death therefore what is earthly
in you: sexual immorality, impurity, passion, evil desire, and
covetousness, which is idolatry. On account of these the wrath
of God is coming. In these you too once walked, when you were
living in them. But now you must put them all away: anger,
wrath, malice, slander, and obscene talk from your mouth.
(**Colossians 3:1–8**), **CSB**.

Colossians is one of the prison epistles that was written by the
Apostle Paul. Even though he had never visited this church, he
was made aware of a heresy that was growing among its believers
and felt obligated to address it. The heresy claimed that Jesus was
a created being, therefore denying His deity. The problem with this
way of thinking is that it lowers the view of Jesus and removes Him
from His proper place of worship.

Is this not what we do in the United States today? As a nation, we
do not see Jesus for who He really is. In doing so, we have lowered
Him in our minds and replaced Him with something else. This is
called idolatry.

I have heard people say that the United States is no longer a religious
nation. I disagree. I think we are very spiritual. Idolatry is an
extremely religious activity. In chapter 5, we talked about the fact
that everyone worships something. It is impossible not to. While
most people in our country no longer worship God, they worship
something else in His place.

Verse 2 of our passage instructs us to *"set our minds on the things*
above." Paul knows that when we put our full attention on earthly
things, they can easily take God's place in our lives. We need to be
aware that anything can become an idol if we let it. Ironically, we
are told to "set our minds," but even they can become idols. This is
a massive problem we face in the United States.

In her book *Love Thy Body*, Nancy Pearcey claims that we have elevated the mind above all else, thereby making it an idol: "Today, we treat the material world—including the body—largely as a construction of the human mind. There is no created order that we are morally obligated to honor or respect. Consciousness determines what is real for us."[25]

The eighteenth-century philosopher Immanuel Kant once said, "What your mind thinks is real, is real." He thought that believing something in your mind was the only requirement for truth. There are dangerous consequences when we go down this road.

Idolizing the mind has caused us to lower the value of the body. Think about what is said of the body: "You can have sex with as many people as you want. Just don't give away your heart." This way of thinking makes the body simply a tool to be used for pleasure. We are taught that having sex with someone is not giving ourselves away. That only happens when we fall in love.

Another thing said is, "Whatever gender you think you are is what you are." It is now our minds that determine our sex, not our anatomy. The transgender community faces serious physical and mental problems over this kind of thinking. These individuals need help and, sadly, we are enabling them to further damage themselves.

A bulimic person looks in the mirror and sees someone overweight. The worst thing we could say to them is, "You know, you're right. You are fat. Continue to starve yourself." That reaction would be the most unloving thing we could say to them. It is the same with a transgendered person. Encouraging them to mutilate their bodies is the most unloving thing we can do for a person who needs help.

When we solely focus on the mind, it causes us to be out of balance. God created us with mind, body, and soul, and He wants us to

25 Pearcey, Nancy. *Love Thy Body*, p. 165.

give the proper attention to each of them. Elevating the mind at the expense of the body and soul makes us unbalanced.

A car operates similarly. There are certain fluids that the driver needs to be aware of: oil, coolant, and gas. If you run out of oil, your engine can seize up. If you run out of coolant, your engine will overheat. If you run out of gas, your car will not go anywhere. Overlooking, or forgetting, any of these three fluids affects the entire car. In the same way, we keep watch over the fluid balance of our vehicles, we need to maintain balance in our lives.

Is it any wonder that our country is facing a mental health crisis? Our lack of balance has caused damage to every aspect of our being. Our teenagers and college students are encouraged to be sexually promiscuous, resulting in the most anxious and depressed generation in our nation's history. The transgender community faces a suicide rate higher than any other group. We are the wealthiest nation in the history of mankind, yet so many Americans struggle with addiction.

Are you in balance? Are you taking the time to nurture your mind, body, and soul? This happens when we live life the way God intended. Paul encouraged the Colossian church to "put to death the earthly things inside us." Focusing on God is the best way to focus on yourself. God created our minds, bodies, and souls. He knows the conditions in which we operate best. Is your mind focused on the things of God? Are you taking care of your body? Are you being fed spiritually with a daily quiet time? Let us not idolize things by putting them above God.

SAY NO TO PRIDE

Therefore, as God's chosen ones, holy and dearly loved, put on compassion, kindness, humility, gentleness and patience,

> *bearing with one another and forgiving one another if anyone has a grievance against another. Just as the Lord has forgiven you, so you are also to forgive.* (**Colossians 3:12–13**), **CSB**.

J.K. Rowling is the famous author who wrote the popular *Harry Potter* series. Each book has been made into a movie resulting in millions of dollars at the box office. She is one of the richest women in the world and has a following of loyal supporters.

In June of 2020, Rowling came under fire when she retweeted an op-ed article that made the statement, "people who menstruate." She took exception to the way the piece was written as it implied that people, other than women, could menstruate. The backlash she faced was severe. Her seemingly uncontroversial claim that only biological women could menstruate angered many of her fans leading them to disown her. People were calling on this celebrity, who was once adored by the public and could do no wrong, to be canceled.

This phenomenon is called "Cancel Culture." It is happening daily. I began this book by discussing the division we are seeing in our country today. This lack of unity has resulted in people trying to silence anyone they disagree with. If a person writes or says anything that contradicts mainstream culture, there is a wave of opposition against that person. It can be something said recently or way back in the past.

The comedian Kevin Hart posted something on social media years ago that resurfaced after he agreed to host the Oscars. Many people were offended, and the Oscars faced pressure to fire him from hosting. They boycotted his movies trying to prevent him from getting work in the future. Hart tried to resolve the situation with an apology, but the backlash was fierce.

Our lack of unity prevents us from forgiving one another. Even an apology is not enough anymore. Public shaming happens with the intention of eradicating the opposing view. What is it that causes so many people to lash out like this? What causes so many people to reject an apology?

In Colossians 3, Paul addresses the growing divisions that were happening within the church. Like our country, there was growing dissent with no reconciliation. These are things that should not be happening in the body of Christ. Sadly, not much has changed. The American Church still struggles with infighting. We let problems with one another go unresolved. The same problem that is wrecking our country is wrecking the Church. That problem is pride.

Pride is what prevents you from apologizing. It tells you that you are the most important, that you are always right. Pride is what stops you from admitting you were wrong. Pride is the opposite of Christianity and it prohibits you from forgiving others. It is a devastating problem within the church that needs to be addressed. We are limiting our effectiveness in the world by portraying a warped view of what the Church should be. Sheldon Vanauken once said:

> The best argument for Christianity is Christians: their joy, their certainty, their completeness. But the strongest argument against Christianity is also Christians—when they are somber and joyless, when they are self-righteous and smug in complacent consecration, when they are narrow and repressive, then Christianity dies a thousand deaths.

We misrepresent Christ when we do not forgive. Paul reminds us that we are to forgive because God forgave us. We are never more like Christ than when we forgive. This means we have to treat others the way Jesus did. It means we need to let go of anger that leads to hate.

To illustrate this point, I want you to think of a rope. One end of the rope represents you and the other end represents a friend or family member. The entire rope represents your relationship with one another. When things are going well, the rope is straight. However, when a fight or argument happens, a knot is tied in the rope. The knot now stands in between the two of you and prevents you from growing closer to one another.

To preserve the relationship, the knot must be untied to make the rope straight again. What happens, though, when you refuse to untie the knot? The knot becomes tighter and tighter as you both pull against one another. At some point, the knot will become so tight that it cannot be untied. The only way to remove the knot is to cut it off, thereby ending the relationship.

Forgiveness is not only a benefit within the Church body. It is one of our greatest tools for sharing Christ with the world around us. Since the start of the early Church, after the death of Jesus on the cross, over seventy million Christians have been killed in the name of Christ. They gave up their lives to proclaim the truth of the Gospel. Many of their deaths were gruesome and barbaric.

Volumes of books have been dedicated to telling their stories. Having read some of them, I am amazed at the number of times I heard the phrase, "Father, forgive them." No matter how unthinkable the death or torture, believers would respond with forgiveness. They pray for the very people who opposed them. This is clearly the work of the indwelling Holy Spirit.

While Stephen, the first recorded martyr, was being stoned, he prayed that God would forgive his murderers. Responding this way is unbelievable to those who do not have a relationship with the Lord. They do not understand. It makes sense though that Jesus, the foundation of our faith, modeled how we are to respond while dying on the cross: *"Father, forgive them, for they know not what they do."*

This way of thinking should dwell within every believer. A.M. Hunter once said, "To return evil for good is the Devil's way; to return good for good is man's way; to return good for evil is God's way." When we hold on to anger, are we acting like Christ? When we refuse to let go of our pride, do we resemble the believers who have come before us and laid down their lives?

Christians, we have to learn to say no to pride. Are you letting it stand in the way of forgiving someone in your life? It is impossible to grow in your relationship with God if you cannot let go of pride. It is impossible to live the abundant life promised in Scripture when you cannot release your anger. Take a moment and think of anyone within the church that you need to forgive. Then, take another moment and think about someone outside of the church. Perhaps your forgiveness could be the thing that points them to Christ.

SAY NO TO THE PAST

When Christ, who is your life, appears, then you also will appear with Him in glory. (**Colossians 3:4**), **CSB.**

Christians are defined by their future, not by their past. One day, we will leave this world and be with God for eternity. We will reunite with all the saints who have come before. There will be no more pain. We get the honor of glorifying Jesus forever. The Bible tells us that this is what should give us our hope.

Unfortunately, many Christians miss out on the abundant life because they focus too much on their past. They look back instead of ahead. We cannot fully live for God if we are letting past mistakes dictate how we act. I have met so many people who seek redemption from God but are unable to forgive themselves. This way of thinking allows your past to stop you from doing what God desires for you. Our hope in what lies ahead should define everything we do. C.S. Lewis once said, "If you read history you will find that the Christians who did most for the present world were just those who thought most of the next."

My biggest fear is that I am going to look back at my life and wish I had done more, that I will see a life of missed opportunities. I want to have the greatest impact for Christ that I can. I heard a local pastor once say, "Younger people are more concerned with destiny while older people are concerned with legacy." What is the legacy you are leaving behind? What lasting impact will you leave on the world?

My friend was telling me a story of how he was watching a football game with his fifteen-year-old son. During the game, my friend commented that he did not really like one of the quarterbacks playing because he was estranged from his family. My friend's son looked over at him and asked, "When's the last time you talked to your dad?"

This question really hit home because my friend had not spoken to his father in over ten years. He was raised Mormon but eventually gave his life to Christ. This caused tension in their relationship. He ended up calling his father and they were able to find a resolution.

About a year later, his father fell in the bathroom and hit his head causing a brain bleed. He died a week later. I remember talking to my friend to see how he was doing. He said, "Obviously, my heart is broken that my dad is gone. However, imagine how I would be feeling if we hadn't made things right a year ago."

My friend is convinced that God spoke to him through his son during that football game. It caused him to see that it does not matter what happened in the past. It does not matter what hurtful words were said. God desires forgiveness. If my friend had dwelled in the past, it would have prevented him from restoring the relationship with his father.

SUFFERING

I cannot finish a chapter about the abundant life without addressing one of the main challenges faced by the believer and non-believer alike: the topic of suffering. With so many Christians being taught that the abundant life leads to earthly happiness free of difficulty, is it any wonder that we see so much doubt in the church when someone faces suffering?

This way of thinking is very prevalent with non-believers. In fact, suffering is often the largest obstacle to overcome when becoming a Christian. There have been endless debates on why God would allow someone to suffer. Why God would allow such evil to occupy this world. Why He would allow natural disasters to take the lives of so many innocent people. This argument, used by many atheists to disprove God, is known as the "problem of evil." The argument goes like this:

Premise 1: If God is all-powerful, he is able to prevent suffering.

Premise 2: If God is all-loving, he wants to prevent suffering.

Premise 3: Evil and suffering exist.

Conclusion: Either God is not all-powerful or he is not all-loving.

Based on the three premises listed above, it makes sense how someone can come to this conclusion. Either God does not exist, or He couldn't care less about His creation. I have met numerous people who cannot get past this argument, preventing them from giving their lives to God. If I am being honest, I am very sympathetic to these people. I have struggled with some of these same questions, even as a believer. There have been moments where I found it difficult to trust a God who could allow such evil things to happen.

Is this what happens though? Do we live in a world in which God has totally removed Himself? There can be an argument made for why God would allow evil to happen to those who reject Him, but what about those who have made Him their Lord? What about Christians? Is it possible to live an abundant life that involves suffering? Look at the theistic argument that refutes the problem of evil:

Premise 1: God is all-loving.

Premise 2: God is all-powerful.

Premise 3: Evil and suffering exist.

Conclusion: God must have a reason for allowing evil and suffering to exist.

God uses suffering and evil to accomplish a greater good, even if we never know exactly what that reason is. I will admit, this is one of the hardest aspects of following Christ. However, I believe this is difficult only for believers who accept the lie that all your problems will go away once you become a Christian. This is found nowhere in Scripture. In fact, the Bible says the opposite. We are told that we will face suffering. We are told that difficult situations will come to those who live for His glory.

1 Peter 4:12–13 says, *"Dear friends, don't be surprised when the fiery ordeal comes among you to test you, as if something unusual were happening to you. Instead, rejoice as you share in the sufferings of Christ, so that you may also rejoice with great joy when his glory is revealed."*

This passage is not found in the small print. This is not something that the early Church avoided or kept secret. Let me be perfectly clear: if you live a life for Jesus Christ, you will face hardship. Your life will not be easy.

The redefinition of the abundant life has many Christians seeking a life that is not promised by God. One could instead make the argument that a life apart from God is the more comfortable life. I always tell people that if you are not facing any kind of persecution for the sake of Christ, you are probably not putting yourself out there enough. You are probably not living fully for Jesus. Here are two things to remember when you inevitably face suffering:

1. God is concerned more with your character than your comfort.
2. Remember who is in control.

Suffering is intended to lead to someone's growth. Many people have given their lives to Christ based on what they witnessed from a believer. The early Church grew at rapid rates because Christians were willing to lay down their lives to proclaim the Gospel. Suffering, in this case, led to the spiritual life, and growth, of those who were once spiritually dead.

Suffering also leads to the growth of the believer. Our godly character tends to grow during uncomfortable times. Scripture is packed full of stories of those who followed God during difficulties. The story of Joseph is a perfect example (Genesis 37–50).

Joseph was his father's favorite son. Out of jealousy, his brothers first threw Joseph in a pit and later sold him into slavery. Joseph still trusted in God. After getting to Egypt, he was wrongfully thrown into prison for a crime he did not commit. Joseph still trusted in God. After being released from prison, he eventually became the second-in-command behind only the Pharaoh himself. God allowed Joseph to interpret a dream that saved Egypt from a famine. Knowing that Egypt had enough food to survive, Joseph's family went to Egypt in hope of avoiding starvation. It was at this moment that Joseph was able to rescue his family.

If Joseph had not been sold into slavery, his family would have perished. If Joseph had not endured the suffering he faced, his family would have starved. Joseph never wavered in his trust for the Lord. He believed that God is always in control. We should never allow our suffering to become bigger than God. Suffering is great at making itself look unbeatable; however, suffering is also great at throwing you into the arms of an all-loving God.

Do not waste the hardships that come your way. They are doing something. Allow suffering to grow your character. Allow it to throw you into the arms of God. Allow it to make your witness stronger. Do not buy into the lie that God is out to get you when you face hard times. Some of the godliest people are the ones who have experienced hell on earth. Suffering, in their case, did not make them doubt God. It made their praises louder.

TAKE ACTION

Take a moment and write down some of the hardest times in your life. Make note of the times when it was hardest to trust in God. Now take a moment to see if any good came out of those hardships. Did you grow in your relationship with God? Did you learn any spiritual lessons that have impacted your life since then? Keeping a journal is a great practice as it helps capture your thoughts during the storms of life. It also gives you the ability to look back and see how God has moved throughout your journey.

IN REVIEW

1. The word NO is necessary to have the abundant life the Bible promises to believers.

2. In the same way that a guardrail prevents you from running your car off the road, God's boundaries, or rules, are set up to help us stay the course.

3. When we solely focus on the mind, it causes us to be out of balance.

4. Are you in balance? Are you taking the time to nurture your mind, body, and soul?

5. Pride is what prevents you from apologizing.

6. We misrepresent Christ when we do not forgive.

7. Christians are defined by their future, not their past.

8. God is concerned more with your character than your comfort.

9. Remember who is in control.

10. Do not waste the hardships that come your way. They are doing something. Allow suffering to grow your character. Allow it to throw you into the arms of God.

Be reDefined

"To talk with God, no breath is lost. Talk on! To walk with God, no strength is lost. Walk on! To wait on God, no time is lost. Wait on!"

E. Stanley Jones

Let us not get tired of doing good, for we will reap at the proper time if we don't give up. (**Galatians 6:9**), **CSB**.

BOOTS ON THE GROUND

The purpose of this book is not to redefine Christianity; it is the opposite. I want us to see it correctly. I want us to see it as the Bible defines it. My desire is that we are led by the power of the Holy Spirit to show the world an accurate picture of Jesus Christ. Let us be honest with ourselves and admit that this is something the American Church is not doing well.

Many of us are committing identity theft. We do not see the Bible as the source of truth. We are not willing to give everything. We tolerate and have a low view of sin. Many Christians live lifestyles that do not demonstrate Jesus is worthy. We refuse to call out the sin in other believers. We lack the motivation to take the Gospel out to those who need to hear it. We are missing out. Missing out on the abundant life that God desires for us. Our country desperately needs a better brand of Christianity. One that lines up with the Scripture.

Have you ever heard the phrase, "boots on the ground"? It was originally a military term. There are times when it is necessary to have a physical presence within a war zone. Having armed soldiers, or "boots on the ground", is often needed to be victorious.

This phrase is also often used when politicians are campaigning. Having boots on the ground refers to the volunteers going out into the neighborhoods and knocking on doors, handing out flyers, making phone calls, etc. These volunteers are having a presence in the community. The communities and neighborhoods are the battlegrounds in which they are trying to win or occupy.

Christians need to have this same mindset. We must be present in the war zone. We have lost the culture because we are absent from it. We need to put boots on the ground. It is sad to me that so many believers think we can make a difference from a distance. If we want to win the culture for Christ, we need to be in it. We need to be a part of it while remaining separate from it. We are at war, yet we refuse to fight on the battlefield.

In an earlier chapter, I spoke of the need to abandon the thought that legislative victory is going to change our culture. Bill Witcherman famously said, "Politics is downstream of culture." This statement shows us the order of priority. We cannot change the culture through politics. Politics is the result of cultural belief. Culture has shaped how our government currently looks.

Legislation may change or prevent action; it cannot change the heart. While I believe laws and punishments for breaking those laws are necessary, the Christian mindset should be more about changing the hearts of unbelievers. It is not enough to simply pass a bill. We must encourage a change in nature. This happens only when someone comes to know Christ as their Savior. We need to get out there. We need to have conversations. We need to show biblical love to those in desperate need of it.

Let me ask a scary question. What would happen to the Church if America was to lose all of its religious freedoms? As terrifying as it sounds, the Church would probably grow. Think about it. The early Church had no religious liberty. They faced great persecution. Yet, the faith grew at rates we have never seen in America. I will be honest; I want to preserve the freedoms we have in this country. However, that is not what I find my confidence in. I am confident in the hope I have in Christ:

> *Therefore, we do not give up. Even though our outer person is being destroyed, our inner person is being renewed day by day. For our momentary light affliction is producing for us an absolutely incomparable eternal weight of glory. So, we do not focus on what is seen, but on what is unseen. For what is seen is temporary, but what is unseen is eternal.* **(2 Corinthians 4:16–18), CSB.**

No matter what we face, our hope does not change. Freedom or not, we have eternity waiting for us on the other side of the grave. The world can never take that away from us, and we must never forget that. I encourage protecting religious freedoms, but we must realize that we may lose them someday. Prepare yourself. How will you respond if that happens?

PARENTING

One of the most overlooked ways of having boots on the ground is through parenting. I am discouraged at how spiritually unprepared our young people are when they leave the home. Many of them go off to college only to have everything they have ever known challenged.

Due to weak and underdeveloped faiths, they abandon God. They turn to the "truths" of this world.

Christian parents need to put in the work and realize that their primary mission field is right in front of them. Remember, God has put us in certain places surrounded by certain people. If you have children, God has placed them in your care to be their primary spiritual influence. Imagine what would happen, imagine the impact on our culture, if Christian parents evangelized to their children.

Paul David Tripp compares parents to ambassadors:

> Ambassador is the perfect word for what God has called parents to be and to do. The only thing an ambassador does, if he's interested in keeping his job, is to faithfully represent the message, methods, and character of the leader who has sent him. He is not free to think, speak, or act independently. The ambassador does not represent his own interest, his own perspective, or his own power.[26]

The biggest excuse I hear from parents is that they do not know the Bible. This is why many of them hand over their spiritual influence to the youth or children's pastor of their church. This is why I said we need to put in the hard work. If you do not know the Bible, learn it. If you do not have a daily quiet time with the Lord, can you really expect your children to develop one?

Deuteronomy 11:18–19 says, *"Imprint these words of mine on your heart and minds, bind them as a sign on your hands, and let them be a symbol on your foreheads. Teach them to your children, talking about them when you sit in your house and when you walk along the road, when you lie down and when you get up."*

This passage tells us the importance of learning the truth of Scripture. We are to know it. We are to be so focused on God's Word that it

---

26 Tripp, Paul David. *Parenting*, p. 14.

impacts every aspect of our lives. Notice that parents are to first internalize the Word before they teach it to their children. It is similar to the instructions received when flying on an airplane. A flight attendant always tells the parents, in case of an emergency, to first put the airbag on themselves before they tend to their children. Parents cannot help their children breathe if they, themselves, are oxygen deprived.

Parents teach their children to love the Word when they love the Word first. Do not miss opportunities to tell your children about God. Pray with them. Read a passage of Scripture while eating dinner. Tell them stories of godly heroes who have come before us. Discuss what is happening in the world and teach them how to see life through a Christian lens.

We parents have a short time to prepare our children for the sinful world that is waiting to devour them. The Devil is ready to attack our children, and we must make every effort to prepare them for the assaults.

OTHER PARTS OF THE BODY

In chapter 6, we discussed love within the Church. Every believer is a part of that body. Sadly, it is hard to see this with all the division that resides within the Church. Did you know that there are over two hundred distinct U.S. Christian denominations? I believe this is the result of how easy it is to be a Christian in the United States. If a certain denomination does not fit your preference, find or start another denomination that does.

I will say, though, I do not believe that the number of denominations necessarily leads to division. Many times, it is just merely differing views on secondary biblical issues (Baptism, worship style, spiritual gifts, etc.). Separate denominations can still be united while having disagreements over issues in the Bible that are not primary. Greg Koukl says, "The main things are the plain things." His point is that

Christianity has core doctrines that are essential to the faith. They are plainly laid out in Scripture.

1. God is the creator of the universe (Genesis 1).

2. Jesus took the penalty for our sins and rose again so that we can be forgiven (Luke 24:46; Mark 16:6)._

3. Jesus lived a perfect and sinless life (Hebrews 4:15).

4. Jesus is the Son of God and equal to God (John 1:1; Luke 22:70).

5. We cannot earn salvation on our own merit (Ephesians 2:8–9).

6. The Bible is the inspired Word of God (Romans 10:17).

7. The Exclusivity of Christ (John 14:6; 1 Timothy 2:5).

8. The Trinity (Genesis 1:26, 1 Corinthians 8:6; 2 Corinthians 13:14).

9. Jesus will one day return (Matthew 24:27; Hebrews 9:28).

These are things that cannot be disputed as they are plainly laid out in Scripture. As the Body of Christ, we need to unite around these things. The secondary issues are definitely worth discussing but not worth dividing over. We have to stop making the secondary issues the main ones. I believe the Devil gets a victory when this happens. He does not want us uniting over the truth that leads to the salvation of lost souls. We have to start acting as one body. We must realize that other parts of the Church body may have different views on certain topics. That is OK. Discuss them without dissent. One of the first steps to taking back the culture is for us to come together and defeat our common enemy.

BE REDEFINED

One night, my wife and I were counseling a young couple that was interested in getting married. They first wanted to address some of the issues they were having in their relationship. We sat around my dinner table and let them share their problems. As I sat there listening,

I was trying my best to think of the spiritual advice I should give. I wanted to give practical steps that would fix all their problems so they could move past them and get married.

When they finished speaking, I leaned forward to ask them some questions, to get some more information before I advised them. After getting more details, my wife Brittany jumped in with her own question. It was for the young lady. She asked, "Do you have a relationship with the Lord? Have you given your life to Christ?" She was quick to answer. She replied with, "No. Not yet."

I sat silent. I was about to give counsel to these two not knowing the most basic piece of information. I was going to advise them to do things in accordance with Scripture. How could I tell her to do spiritual things if she had no relationship with God? I was amazed that my wife asked this question because it never occurred to me that I was speaking with someone who did not love Jesus. Ever since that night, I now begin all of my counseling sessions with that question.

It would be wrong for me to assume that everyone reading this book is fully sold out for Christ. We are all in different stages of sanctification. Maybe you are reading this, and you have been living a counterfeit Christianity, one that looks different from how the Bible describes it. Ask yourself the question my wife asked: Have you given your life to Jesus?

I am not asking if you go to church. I am not asking if you read your Bible. Plain and simple, do you live your life for the glory of Christ? If you are honest and your answer is no, my advice for you is to be redefined. This, however, is not something you can do on your own. It is easy for someone to read this book and say, "Oh, here is a list of things I need to accomplish to be a good Christian." That is the wrong mindset.

The first step is to surrender to Christ. Let Him redefine who you are. He is the only one who can do it. Without Him, you are a sinful creature who is spiritually dead. You are a slave to sin. It is only when we are saved by the sacrificial blood of Jesus Christ that we become something different. We are no longer defined as sinful and dead; we are alive and free. 2 Corinthians 5:17 says, *"Therefore, if anyone is in Christ, he is a new creation; the old has passed away, and see, the new has come."*

Perhaps you are reading this book and you do love the Lord; however, the Christian life you are living does not look like the early Church. It does not look anything like the life of Christ. In that case, your spiritual walk requires redefinition.

We are living in a time when true Christianity is absolutely necessary. When believers who fully love Jesus need to stand up and live on mission. We cannot sugarcoat it. We are walking uphill. We have a long road ahead of us, but we must never tire. We must never give up doing good in the name of Jesus Christ.

THE VOICE WITHIN

The next step is often difficult. Every part of your earthly nature is seeking to keep you away from God. The Devil does not want you to live for Christ. He does not want you to have an abundant life in which you live in complete freedom from sin. This voice within is fighting with everything it has. It will try to deceive you with lies. It will attempt to make you think you are something you are not.

"You are a failure."

"You cannot do this."

"You will never live up to the Christian standards."

"God could never forgive someone like you."

Realize that the attacks are coming and prepare yourself with the truth of Scripture. Do not allow the enemy to have victory. Jesus did all the work. He paid the price on your behalf. Jesus suffered and died because He believed you are worth it.

Let me conclude this book with one last story involving my children. My daughter Maura and my son Jack really enjoy making art. They spend hours drawing and painting. There is a room in our house that is dedicated to arts and crafts.

My wife had been teaching them about Vincent Van Gogh and had shown them some of his work. My children loved learning about him and the impact he had on western art (Fun fact: Did you know that Van Gogh only sold one painting in his entire life? He only found fame after his death).

My wife challenged my kids to paint a picture in the same style as Van Gogh. They were up for the challenge. Maura painted a picture similar to "Starry Night," one of Van Gogh's most famous works. She spent a lot of time on it. When she eventually finished, she was disappointed. It did not look the way she wanted it to. My wife tried to encourage her, but Maura was not having it. She felt she had created a terrible piece of art.

She took the painting, walked over to the trash, and threw it away. "I'm a terrible painter," she said. Then she went to her room. She was obviously very upset with herself and no amount of encouragement from my wife or other children could convince Maura that she was not a horrible artist.

The next day, Maura went up into her bedroom to get something. There, sitting on her bed, was the painting that she had thrown in the trash. On top of it was a note written by my son. It said, "You're a good painter Maura. From Jack."

My son had gone into the trash to retrieve the painting she had discarded. He proved to his sister that her work was not garbage and that she was a good painter. The reality is that the painting was really good. She had done a great job, but she convinced herself otherwise. She was believing lies about herself that were not true. My son had not only told her she was a good painter; he showed her with action.

This is the same reason we should never believe the lies of the enemy. God does not just tell us of His love, He showed us. On the cross, Christ proved His love for us and that He sees us as beloved sons and daughters no matter what we think of ourselves.

We do not deserve what Christ did for us. Every believer knows this. It is our job to spread this news and stop keeping it to ourselves. We need to live up to what God has called us to be. We are not called to be a church of hypocrites. We are not called to be silent. Let us live by the truth, take up arms, and make an impact on the world by being the church God desires us to be.

TAKE ACTION

Write out some practical steps you are going to take after reading this book. Is there anything in your spiritual walk that you need to change? What are some ways in which you can be bold about your faith?

IN REVIEW

1. We have lost the culture because we are absent from it.
2. We cannot change the culture through politics. Politics is the result of cultural belief.
3. No matter what we face, our hope doesn't change.

4. Freedom or not, we have eternity waiting for us on the other side of the grave.

5. Due to weak and underdeveloped faiths, our youth are abandoning God.

6. If you have children, God has placed them in your care to be their primary spiritual influence.

7. The Devil is ready to attack our children, and we must make every effort to prepare them for the assaults.

8. The secondary issues are definitely worth discussing but not worth dividing over.

9. One of the first steps to taking back the culture is for us to come together and defeat our common enemy.

10. We have a long road ahead of us, but we must never tire. We must never give up doing good in the name of Jesus Christ.

Bibliography

1. Alexander, T. D. (2009). *From Eden to the new Jerusalem: An introduction to biblical theology*. Grand Rapids, MI: Kregel Academic & Professional.

2. Chan, F. (2018). *Letters to the Church*. Colorado Springs, CO: David C. Cook.

3. Dickerson, J. S. (2013). *The great evangelical recession: 6 factors that will crash the American church—and how to prepare*. Grand Rapids, MI: Baker Books.

4. Elmore, T. (2012). *Habitudes: Images that form leadership habits & attitudes*. Atlanta, GA: Growing Leaders.

5. Erickson, M. J. (1984). *Christian theology*. Grand Rapids, MI: Baker.

6. Grudem, W. A. (1994). *Systematic theology: An introduction to Biblical doctrine*. Leicester, Great Britain: IVP.

7. Kauflin, B. (2008). *Worship matters leading others to encounter the greatness of God*. Wheaton, IL: Good News.

8. Kellemen, B., & Tripp, P. (2015). *Biblical Counseling And The Church: God's Care Through God's People*. Grand Rapids, MI: Zondervan.

9. Keller, T. (2016). *The prodigal God: Recovering the heart of the Christian faith*. New York, NY: Penguin Books.

10. Koukl, G. (2017). *The story of reality: How the world began, how it ends, and everything important that happens in between*. Grand Rapids, MI: Zondervan.

11. Koukl, G. (2019). *Tactics: A game plan for discussing your Christian convictions*. Grand Rapids, MI: Zondervan Reflective.

12. Lane, T. S., & Tripp, P. D. (2008). *How people change*. Greensboro, NC: New Growth Press.

13. Lewis, C. S. (2012). *The Complete C.S. Lewis Signature Classics*. London, UK: Collins.

14. Lundgaard, K. (1998). *The enemy within: Straight talk about the power and defeat of sin*. Phillipsburg, NJ: P & R.

15. MacArthur, J. (1983). *The ultimate priority: John Macarthur, Jr. on worship*. Chicago, IL: Moody Press.

16. Pearcey, N. (2008). *Total truth: Liberating Christianity from its cultural captivity*. Wheaton, IL: Crossway Books.

17. Pearcey, N. (2019). *Love thy body: Answering hard questions about life and sexuality*. Grand Rapids, MI: Baker Books.

18. Schaeffer, F. A. (2011). *True Spirituality*. Carol Stream, IL: Tyndale House.

19. Tripp, P. D. (2016). *Parenting: The 14 gospel principles that can radically change your family*. Wheaton, IL: Crossway.

20. Walsh, M. (2020). *Church of cowards: A wake-up call to complacent Christians*. Washington, DC: Regnery Gateway.

21. Walsh, M. (2020). *Church of cowards: A wake-up call to complacent Christians*. Washington, DC: Regnery Gateway.

22. Whitney, D. S. (2014). *Spiritual disciplines for the Christian life*. Colorado Springs, CO: NavPress.

CPSIA information can be obtained
at www.ICGtesting.com
Printed in the USA
BVHW081314160921
616891BV00002B/253

9 781954 618183